Tartuffe

Molière (1622–73) was born Jean-Baptiste Poquelin, son of a prosperous upholsterer of Paris. Molière was meant to succeed his father in the service of the King. However, in 1643 he changed his surname and joined a family of actors, the Béjarts. Encouraged by their touring success the group returned to Paris and performed in front of Louis XIV and his Court. The success of his farce *Le Docteur Amoureux* gave the group the opportunity to share a theatre at the Petit-Bourbon with an Italian company, and here Molière's reputation was established. His plays include *L'Ecole des Femmes* (1662), *Don Juan* (1665), *Tartuffe* (written 1664, produced 1669), *Le Misanthrope* (1666), *Le Bourgeois Gentilhomme* (1671), *Les Femmes Savantes* (1673) and *Le Malade Imaginaire* (1673).

John Donnelly's plays include *Bone* (Royal Court Theatre), *Corporate Rock* (Nabokov/Latitude Festival), *Conversation #1* (The Factory/V&A/Latitude Festival/ SGP), *Songs of Grace and Redemption* (Liminal Theatre/ Theatre503), *Encourage the Others* (Almeida Lab), *Burning Bird* (Synergy/Unicorn Theatre), *The Knowledge* (Bush), a version of Anton Chekhov's *The Seagull* (Headlong) and *The Pass* (Royal Court Theatre).

T0322532

also by John Donnelly from Faber

BONE
SONGS OF GRACE AND REDEMPTION
THE KNOWLEDGE
THE SEAGULL
THE PASS

MOLIÈRE

Tartuffe
THE IMPOSTER

in a new version by
JOHN DONNELLY

from a literal translation by
Guillaume Pigé

FABER & FABER

First published in 2019
by Faber and Faber Limited
The Bindery, 51 Hatton Garden
London EC1N 8HN

Typeset by Country Setting, Kingsdown, Kent CT14 8ES
Printed in England by CPI Group (UK) Ltd, Croydon CR0 4YY

A CIP record for this book
is available from the British Library

978-0-571-35435-1

Printed and bound in the UK on FSC® certified paper in line with our continuing
commitment to ethical business practices, sustainability and the environment.
For further information see faber.co.uk/environmental-policy

6 8 10 9 7

For my mother, who lied, and lied well

Thank yous

Chris Campbell
Dr Clare Finburgh
Kara Fitzpatrick
Lisa Foster
Frances Grey
Joe Hill-Gibbins
Patrick Marber
Dinah Wood

Blanche McIntyre for her ceaseless support
and encouragement, and the entire company
of *Tartuffe* for their wit and invention

Tartuffe in this version was first performed on the
Lyttelton stage of the National Theatre, London,
on 9 February 2019. The cast, in order of speaking,
was as follows:

Pernelle Susan Engel
Elmire Olivia Williams
Cleante Hari Dhillon
Dorine Kathy Kiera Clarke
Damis Enyi Okoronkwo
Mariane Kitty Archer
Orgon Kevin Doyle
Valere Geoffrey Lumb
Tartuffe Denis O'Hare
Loyal Matthew Duckett
Officer Henry Everett
Ensemble Adeyinka Akinrinade, Nathan Armarkwei-
    Laryea, Fayez Bakhsh, Will Kelly, Penelope McGhie,
    Kevin Murphy, Roisin Rae, Dominik Tiefenthaler

Director Blanche McIntyre
Set and Costume Designer Robert Jones
Lighting Designer Oliver Fenwick
Composition and Sound Design Ben and Max Ringham
Physical Comedy Director Toby Park
Company Voice Work Jeannette Nelson
Staff Director Ed Madden

Characters

in order of speaking

Pernelle

Mariane

Cleante

Dorine

Elmire

Damis

Orgon

Valere

Tartuffe

Loyal

Officer

Actions are largely implied from the text.
Occasionally, for clarity, these are specified.

TARTUFFE

Ils n'ont eu garde de l'attaquer par le côté qui
les a blessés: ils sont trop politiques pour cela,
et savent trop bien vivre pour découvrir le fond
de leur âme.

[They have been careful not to attack those elements
that really wound them. They are too sly for that,
smart enough not to reveal what lies deep
in their soul.]

Moliere, from his introduction to *Tartuffe*

*

The liberal deviseth liberal things.
Isaiah 32, 8

This version of the text was correct
at the time of going to press, but may differ
slightly from the play as performed

A period town house in what appears to be modern London – Highgate, to be specific.

Mirrors, places to hide.

As the play opens, the world of the play will look quite normal – almost. Something not quite *right, perhaps you can't put your finger on it.*

By the end the world will be ruptured entirely. This change may be gradual, subtle, barely perceptible, but by the end we will ask ourselves: how did we end up here?

*

Tartuffe shuffles on to the bare stage, in front of the curtain.

You barely notice him to begin with, as he dispenses single flowers to members of the audience, along with small cards – on which are printed his name and the message 'Truth, friend' and a smiley face.

This dumbshow should carry on for longer than is comfortable, long enough to raise the terrifying prospect that Tartuffe may seek to dispense flowers and cards to the entire audience.

A masked, naked man runs across the stage. Tartuffe barely seems to notice, if at all.

Tartuffe closes his eyes, beats a tattoo on his chest, softly, slowly at first, increasing in speed, mouthing a silent prayer as he does so.

The rumble of a party, barely audible, in time with Tartuffe's fist, as if he brings it into being. The rumble closer now, louder. We barely glimpse it. We feel *it.*

*Tartuffe opens his eyes, looks at us – is that a smile? –
and as mysteriously as he took the stage, he is gone.*

*The noise deafening, overwhelming, then suddenly
silent, making way for:*

One

Mariane and Cleante at repose.
  Pernelle enters, pursued by Elmire and Dorine.
  Damis enters shortly after.

Pernelle No, no, no, no, no.

Mariane What's Granny saying this time?

Cleante I can't be sure but I think your grandmother is saying no.

Mariane To what?

Dorine Everything.

Pernelle I cannot and will not stay another moment in this madhouse.

Elmire What exactly is the matter this time?

Pernelle There was a man in my room.

Cleante Don't shout, we'll all want one.

Elmire Why would a man be in your room?

Cleante I know, the mind boggles.

Pernelle I was occupied in the en-suite when I heard a noise.

Elmire What kind of noise?

Pernelle A groan. I ventured out to find him sprawled on my bed.

Dorine Doing what?

Pernelle Decorum prevents me from saying.

Damis What's happening?

Mariane Granny had a strange man in her room.

Damis Well done, Granny.

Pernelle He was not welcome.

Damis Oh, sorry I thought you might have –

Pernelle Damis darling, don't think, certainly not out loud or in company – it gives you the most pained expression as if you're passing something and spoils that lovely face of yours.

Mariane What did this man look like?

Pernelle I couldn't say, I was distracted.

Cleante By what?

Pernelle His person.

Elmire What about his person?

Pernelle That is the point. There was nothing about his person.
 He was fully nude and in a state of partial arousal.

Damis Which part?

Dorine He could still be there, someone should take a look.

Cleante I'll go.

Pernelle I was entirely at his mercy, he could have done anything he wanted.

Elmire And what did he do?

Pernelle He leapt from the window.

Dorine The fall would have killed him!

Pernelle It was broken by a hedge.

Elmire How convenient.

Pernelle Not exactly. He bounced into the pond.

Cleante Ah.

Pernelle Then leapt over the fence and made his escape.

Cleante With you in hot pursuit no doubt.

Pernelle How droll we all are. How pleased with our inconsequence.

Elmire No harm was done.

Pernelle No harm! Sexual deviants charging about the place willy-nilly.

Elmire According to you he was trying to escape.

Pernelle What on earth the neighbours make of these orgies I have no idea.

Elmire Orgies! There are no orgies here, this is Highgate.

Pernelle What would you call them then?

Cleante Soirées.

Mariane Gatherings.

Damis PARTIES!

Cleante Whatever you call them, they're fun, who cares what the neighbours think?

Pernelle Well, I want no part in any of this. I've been telling my son for months this house has gone to seed. I'd intended to tell him to pull his bloody socks up but apparently he's *in the country* – God knows what that's a euphemism for. And it's not just the parties, it's the whole self-congratulatory merry-go-round, you haven't the faintest interest what happens outside your own front door – there's people sleeping on the streets, not that you'd notice. Too busy being seen, attending openings, cavorting with your rugger bugger mates or that awful poet of yours.

Mariane He's a street poet and his name is Valere.

Pernelle I can do without his biography, thank you.
  You're detached, the lot of you, and it'll be your undoing, mark my words.
  I blame you, this wouldn't have happened when their mother was alive. I told my son not to marry you, did he listen? Led by his rod. Thought you were quite the catch when we all know the truth is you were the one playing him, and got yourself landed, I wish he'd thrown you back.
  I said at the time, all she is is decoration, and the problem with decoration is sooner or later the baubles lose their shine.

Elmire Any more metaphors you intend on mixing or are you finished?

Pernelle I'm sorry, is there something you need to be seeing to – or someone perhaps?

Elmire Well I was hoping to polish my baubles.

Pernelle I'll bet you were.
  The only consolation of my entire visit is the prospect that finally there's someone in this household with a modicum of decency.

Cleante Who could she mean?

Mariane Let me think.

Damis It beats me
  No it really does, who does she mean?

Cleante/Dorine/Elmire/Mariane Tartuffe!

Damis Tartuffe, yes, I knew that.

Pernelle That man has more decency in his little finger than the lot of you put together.

Cleante He's a zealot.

Pernelle A zealot is merely someone with principles as described by someone who has none.

Cleante I do so have principles.

Pernelle Yes, a great many, one for every occasion.

Damis Tartuffe is trying to take over.

Pernelle Good, it's about time someone took the reins.

Mariane He's got Daddy wrapped around his finger.

Damis Our stepmother is banned from having visitors.

Pernelle Don't exaggerate, no one's banned.

Mariane He doesn't have to ban them, he's just made it so unbearable, no one wants to show up.

Damis Nearly ruined last night's party with his lecture on spiritual values.

Cleante That was the highlight of my evening! When he started chanting and doing that weird movement of his, I thought he was going to pop!

Dorine What gives him the right to barge in here and do all this?

Pernelle No barging necessary, as you well know, he was invited by my son, whose house this is.

Dorine He's made himself at home all right.

Pernelle I'm sorry, this is a family discussion, I thought you were the help.

Dorine My official title is housekeeper, thank you very much, although I like to think of myself as a little more than that.

Pernelle Oh we all like to think of ourselves as a little 'more than', don't we?

Damis Anyway, he couldn't stop us having last night's party, that showed him who's really in charge.

Pernelle All that's going to change. I have my informers.

Cleante Informers?

Mariane She means Daphne.

Damis What's a Daphne?

Dorine Her across the way.

Elmire You see her at the window, binoculars at the ready, curtains twitching.

Pernelle Daphne is a woman of impeccable character.

Dorine I remember the moment she became a woman of impeccable character. When the offers started drying up, that's when she had her attack of righteousness.

Pernelle What a vicious little thing you are.

Dorine Wasn't so long ago Daphne was the most popular woman this side of the ponds. Then time caught up with her, and now she's not getting any, no one else is allowed any either – like some others I could mention.

Pernelle I'm so pleased you have these tawdry fantasies to fall back on, it must enliven an otherwise torpid existence.
  Where is my son? I was told he was due back.

Elmire Don't ask me, I'm just the decoration.

Pernelle When you see him, tell him from me, he has made many regrettable decisions, some of whom are in this room, but one thing for which I shall remain eternally grateful is bringing in this man Tartuffe.

Last night's act of petty rebellion notwithstanding, he has had an invigorating effect on this household.

Dorine He's had an invigorating effect on someone.

Pernelle One of the benefits of advancing years is no longer having to pretend to give two shits what people think of you.

What's that hollow noise I hear? Oh that's right, it's the sound of your laughter catching in your throats.

You'll learn, everyone has to, that none of this lasts forever.

Pernelle leaves.
Elmire follows – as do Mariane and Damis.

Cleante Is it just me or is she getting nuttier?

Dorine It's not her I'm worried about.

Cleante Orgon. How concerned do you think we need to be?

Orgon appears.

Orgon Concerned about what?

Cleante Where the hell did you spring from?

Orgon Has my mother gone?

Dorine You just missed her.

Cleante How was your business in the country?

Orgon Why, what did you hear?

Elmire enters.

Elmire You're back.

Orgon looks directly at her, then ignores her.

Orgon So how is he?

Cleante How's who?

Elmire He means Tartuffe.

Orgon Well, how is he?

Elmire Why don't you ask him yourself?

Elmire exits.

Orgon What's up with my wife?

Dorine Her migraines have returned.

Orgon But how is Tartuffe?

Dorine He's put on a little weight.

Orgon Oh God, is he all right?

Dorine I would say so, yes, the other night he ate his own meal, then your wife's, then emptied the larder of cheese and was last seen heading for the wine cellar.

Orgon The poor man!

Dorine Your wife hasn't ate or slept in days, at night you can hear her crying throughout the house, three times I've gone in to find her doubled-up in agony, moaning and wailing.

Orgon That's awful. She must be keeping Tartuffe awake.

Dorine Not judging by the volume of the snoring coming from his room, no.

Orgon He needs his rest.

Dorine Well he's certainly getting that. Night before last he washed his meal down with three bottles of your best claret, staggered upstairs, farted a prayer, then passed out on the landing.

Orgon What was the prayer?

Dorine Two 'Hail Marys', an 'Our Father' and for the climax a Buddhist lament.

Orgon Oh God, the poor man!

Dorine The doctor prescribed medication for Elmire's headaches and anxiety.

Orgon So where is he now?

Dorine Back at his surgery.

Orgon Not the doctor, Tartuffe!

Dorine He appeared for breakfast in a kimono that was scarcely there, sank four Bloody Marys then returned to bed, where as far as I know he's been ever since.

Orgon The poor man!

Dorine I'll be sure to tell your wife you were asking after her.

    Dorine exits.

Cleante She's taking the piss out of you, you know that.

Orgon Of course I do, I'm not stupid. But I ignore the complaints of this world. It is the good man's burden to be despised.

Cleante You've started talking like him now. You've even started to dress like him.

Orgon You mean Tartuffe.

Cleante What's got into you – fine, you want to give something back, take someone in off the street, do your bit, that's one thing, but why him?

Orgon That's what bothers you, that he's off the street?

Cleante Of course not.

Orgon Then what?

Cleante The way you are with him it's . . . odd.

Orgon Oh I see, that's the only way you can make sense of it, some tawdry notion.

Cleante For God's sake. Men, women, in between, as if I care – what a married man gets up to in the privacy of his own pied-à-terre is no business of mine.

Orgon I'm not getting up to anything.

Cleante But all this mooning around – Tartuffe this, Tartuffe that – allowing him to dictate the running of the house. How can you be so blinkered?

Orgon Without blinkers the horse doesn't finish the race.

Cleante You're not a horse! And this isn't a race.

Orgon I need to regain my focus, I've paid attention to too many people for too long.

Cleante Focus is one thing, this is an obsession.

Orgon It's not an obsession!

Cleante What do you call it?

Orgon An awakening.

Cleante What is he? A guru, a spiritual advisor?

Orgon A friend.

Cleante Well so am I – your oldest friend, and I'm worried.

Orgon If you only gave him a chance you'd understand the kind of man he is.

Cleante And what kind of man is that?

Orgon A man who – a man who – a man who – a man!

Cleante Well, I'm glad we cleared that up.

Orgon I'm not as clever as you with words, I never have been. What Tartuffe does is . . . inexpressible. He inspires me to be who I am, more than I am, a me I didn't even know existed.

Cleante He's taking you for a ride.

Orgon How? He refuses my money. I tried paying him, he wouldn't take it.

Cleante He eats your food, drinks your wine, he's obsessed with my sister, your wife – remember her? She barely goes out any more and spends most days in her room avoiding him. She used to be so full of life, she's shrinking, that doesn't bother you?

Orgon He's protective.

Cleante He's controlling.

Orgon His concern is my wife's honour –

Cleante Honour! Can you hear yourself? This language, what year do you think this is?
    And it's not her *honour* he's interested in, I assure you.

Orgon It's your eyes are polluted, not his heart.
    You're so immersed in this squalor you can't see the world as it truly is.

Cleante And what is it, truly?

Orgon A dungheap encircled by flies.

Cleante We're the flies, I take it?

Orgon He gives me clarity, purpose. Thanks to Tartuffe, all doubt, all uncertainty has melted away.

Cleante A little uncertainty, a little humility even, is not a bad thing.

Orgon Why can't you be happy for me?

Cleante I don't know who you are any more, you've turned into a totally different person.

Orgon Thank you.

Cleante It's not a compliment! What is this? A mid-life crisis? Why can't you just buy a car, or sleep with one of your daughter's friends like a normal person?

Orgon This is exactly what I mean, this flippancy, it's the default position of the modern age.

Cleante The modern age!

Orgon No one takes anything seriously any more. Values are devalued, people do what they want, live how they like.

Cleante And what's wrong with that, as long as no one is harmed?

Orgon A line must be drawn, before we entirely lose a sense of who we are.

Cleante Honour, values, losing a sense of who we are, what is all this regression, what are you trying to get back to?
    When you and my sister found one another, I was pleased, for both of you, but I admit I was also a little concerned – I didn't want to say it at the time because you seemed so happy. Delirous. So was she. But you were still grieving. It was quick, maybe too quick. I can't help wondering if there was something unsettled in you, even then, something that has taken root and it's manifesting itself in this back-to-basics bullshit.

Orgon Something has taken root, Cleante. It's been building. Change is coming, mark my words, the old orders are falling, out there and now within these walls people are saying 'No more!'

Cleante No more what?

Orgon For some time now, something has sat uneasy within me.
  At first, a feeling, a murmur, a sense something was missing. A nagging voice that grew and grew, until a few months ago the pressure in my head, my chest, I couldn't take it any more. I was in the middle of going over some papers and found myself gripped by a terror – what am I doing? What's it all for? – I stood up, left my desk and walked from the office, no idea where I was going. The sorrow I felt as I looked around me – people begging, hopeless – I walked and walked until I found myself in the most desolate place you can imagine, a place devoid of all joy, all life, no beauty, no humour, just misery and despair in the eyes of everyone around you.

Cleante You walked to Archway?

Orgon I stopped on the overpass, watched the cars speeding below, wondering if I'd ever make it home.

Cleante You never told me this.

Orgon Are you surprised? Everything's a joke to you.
  I kept going and as the shops melted away, I turned into an industrial estate, some unseen force compelled me. A cry came from a clapped-out old Portakabin with a sign in front: 'Truth, friend'.
  Grotty little place. Horrible tablecloths, noticeboards. People scattered here and there, nothing about them – serving food, tea. No ostentation. Just doing good honest work. And at the far end of the room, a very basic makeshift altar, nothing ornate, just . . . straightforward. Simple.
  In front, there were cheap plastic chairs in rows. I sat, overwhelmed by the heaviness that descends before you give in, closed my eyes, silently hoped for a sign.

At first nothing. Of course, nothing, there is nothing, but then, a tingling, a warmth in my heart. I felt a presence. I opened my eyes and there he was.

Cleante Tartuffe?

Orgon No, the caretaker. He needed to clear the chairs away. Of course Tartuffe, that's the point of the bloody story!

Cleante I wasn't meaning to be facetious, I was – carry on, please!

Orgon There he was on his knees, chanting softly, hands clasped, knuckles straining white. With his fist, he began to drum a tattoo on his chest, slow at first, but then faster, his voice rising with each strike, on and on, until finally he let forth moans and groans the like of which I have never heard. I was enraptured. Who was this man? Then suddenly without warning he stopped dead, turned to me, drew my ear close to his mouth, and whispered a single word:
'Reckoning.'
'Reckoning.'
Then, I'll never forget this, he looked directly at me, those eyes of his, piercing me. As if he knew everything I had ever done. And the relief, oh God, to be *known*.
A tide of shame engulfed me.
Drowning in the life I've lived, the things I've done, the endless compromise.
I tried to give him money – my guilt! – he snatched the notes from my hands, tossed them in the air like they were nothing, he was mocking me and I ran. In a frenzy, ran vowing never to go back but that night in my dreams, those eyes – bearing down on me.
The next day I returned, grabbed him like a madman, insisted he join me here, that he may inspire me and I others.

He tried to refuse but I was resolute. Now that I'd found him how could I let him go?

Since then I have put my trust in him and, Cleante, I have opened like a flower to a bee.

You're right, he has transformed me. I am not who I was and if you knew the kind of man he is, you would join me too.

A week ago, we took a stroll on the Heath, a fly buzzed near us, instinctively he clapped his hands and there it was, squashed in his palm. And the sense of loss he felt, the remorse – it broke him, he wept.

Cleante Over a fly?

Orgon Yes, a fly. The compassion of the man! Do you see?

Cleante Finally, I think I do.

Orgon You do, really?

Cleante Yes. You've completely lost your mind.

Orgon I forget, you have all the answers, no wiser man walked the earth.

Cleante I will not abandon my critical faculties at the altar of blind faith.

Orgon You sneer at faith, you always have, you're a slave to your intellect, to people like you belief is a punch-line.

Cleante I have no objection to religion, spirituality, faith, whatever this is, but in moderation.

Orgon And where has your moderation gotten us, look outside these four walls? There are people who want to destroy our way of life, do we tolerate them? All your 'yes, but' and 'on the other hand', this world is in pain and reason cannot heal it.

Cleante This is idiotic!

Orgon I'm an idiot now? That's how you win me round, by insulting me?

Cleante I can't stand by and watch as you push your family away.

Orgon I won't pander to them any longer, that was my mistake.

Cleante You will lose everyone you love, including my sister, including me if you're not careful.

Orgon There is no room for sentiment in my heart, not any more. I would rather kill my family with my own hands than see them continue down this path of self-destruction.

Cleante You're not serious?

Orgon They are suffocating themselves with their lifestyles, killing themselves day by day.
    You know nothing of the world apart from what you read in supplements, you haven't served your country the way I have, seen what I've seen. You think the world is powered by reason, you're naive, what is required is clarity and order.

Cleante At the expense of rational thought?

Orgon A persuasive argument, some *killer fact*, and we all fall into line with what you consider acceptable, that's what you think! That is not how the world runs. It runs on emotion, feeling, that's what drives us, not reason.

Cleante Without reason we are animals.

Orgon We are animals! Why pretend otherwise! We have a need deep within to nurture and protect. To deny that is to deny our true selves! When my first wife – God rest

her soul – was dying I promised I would take care of our children. I failed them. And I failed her.
  When I married your sister it was for selfish reasons.

Cleante Love is not selfish.

Orgon I have been lax. Now my family are lax. Profligate, slovenly, their concerns trivial.

Cleante They're young.

Orgon They're not children any more.

Cleante So why treat them as such?

Orgon I am to blame and I must take responsibility.

Cleante How does handing over all moral authority to Tartuffe square up with taking responsibility?

Orgon He gives them a discipline I cannot provide. That may be my failing, but with Tartuffe's help I can right that wrong.

Cleante What about love? Don't you love your family any more?

Orgon This is love. Real love. Tough love.
  Not the love of nice words, of simpering, of romance.
  A love that is strong, unbending, unafraid to be hated, because it knows itself to be right.

Cleante You're planning something aren't you? What is it?
  What do you have in mind?

Orgon The time for talk is done. I must go.

  Orgon leaves.

Cleante
  His eyes! Full of a zeal he doesn't fully understand.
  All logic and compassion ripped from his hands
  By some unseen force –

You saw! Entirely without remorse.
In times like these, a man like this
Tartuffe can prosper. – If you insist,
Despite the evidence of your eyes,
That right is wrong and black is white,
With enough fervour, you'll be believed,
Because truth is now the poor man's currency.
And that really does worry me, because who knows,
To serve an idea, how far a man like that'll go?

Two

Orgon, Mariane.

Orgon Mariane!

Mariane God, don't do that!

Orgon I didn't mean to startle you.

Mariane You just sort of appeared. You do that a lot at the moment.

Orgon Were you sneaking off somewhere?

Mariane I'm not sneaking anywhere, I was just popping out.

Orgon Where to?

Mariane Out.

Orgon Are you avoiding me?

Mariane Why would I do that?

Orgon There's something I need to talk to you about.

Mariane Ominous.

Orgon Oh no, nothing to, you know – It won't take long. Please.

He indicates 'one moment',
   He checks they are alone.

Mariane Are you all right?

Orgon Walls have ears.

Mariane Ears?

Orgon Eyes too.

Mariane Ears and eyes, gosh.

Orgon Alone.
    Mariane, do you love me?

Mariane What?

Orgon Do you love me?

Mariane Oh my God, are you dying?

Orgon Why would I be dying?

Mariane Asking if I love you.

Orgon Perfectly normal question.

Mariane You've never really been that kind of father. I don't mind. It's just, well, you know, you're a certain sort.

Orgon What sort is that?

Mariane You bottle things up. You've never been one to talk. Or rather you don't talk then suddenly you do and you won't stop and by that time you've pretty much made up your mind anyway, so . . .

Orgon But do you – love me?

Mariane Of course.

Orgon And you know I love you?

Mariane You've not always been the best at expressing it, and I know we've had our difficult patches – like when you met Elmire, I was doubtful at first, because it all seemed so sudden but then you've always been impulsive.

Orgon I always thought I was rather measured.

Mariane Most of the time, but every now and then you sort of pop. You and Mummy were forever waking Damis and me up in the dead of night, bundling us into a car, off on an adventure. I miss that. I think you do too, you've always needed people more than you let on. But yes, to answer your question, I do know you love me, in your own way.

Orgon Good.
Good.
And what do you make of Tartuffe?

Mariane If having him around makes you happy then you always seem to know what's best.
Was that what you wanted to talk about?

Orgon What I really want to talk about is the future.

Mariane The future?

Orgon Your future. You're not a girl any more. You're a young woman.

Mariane You noticed.

Orgon And as a young woman there are things you need to consider that you perhaps haven't considered before.

Mariane This isn't the talk, is it?

Orgon The talk?

Mariane You know, the *talk*. Because I have to say it's a bit late.

Orgon No, no, this isn't the – hang on, what do you mean, 'a bit late'?

Mariane Well I've had boyfriends, I mean what did you think –

Orgon I didn't think. I just assumed – that you'd tell me or something if you were having –

Mariane Sex.

Orgon Yes.

Mariane Why would I tell you?

Orgon So you're saying you have had –

Mariane It's actually none of your business.

Orgon Of course it isn't.

Mariane But as it happens, no, I haven't.

Orgon Oh. Right. Good for you.

Mariane Not really, anyway.

Orgon What does 'Not really' mean?

Mariane I've done bits, obviously.

Orgon Which bits?

Mariane Do you really want to know?

Orgon No, actually, I don't.

Mariane Look, it's not a religious thing. I'm not a prude. I just haven't. You don't have to. A girl's right to choose. And I just wanted to wait. I just thought it would be . . . more romantic. I'm quite old-fashioned that way. Your generation probably thinks that's weird, but we're not all at it.

Orgon Right.
    So you want to get married?

Mariane You know I've always dreamt of a wedding.

Orgon But I'm talking about marriage. Which isn't the same as a wedding.

Mariane No, it's the bit after.

Orgon It's a commitment.

Mariane Yes.

Orgon You have to make sure you marry the right person.

Mariane Obviously.

Orgon Let's talk about what that might mean. For you.

Mariane Well. It means Valere.

Orgon Valere.

Mariane Yes, Valere.

Orgon The poet.

Mariane Street poet.

Orgon I'm still not sure what that is.

Mariane Well, it's –

Orgon I'm not really asking – what I am asking is what qualities you would look for in a husband, think about it in the abstract.

Mariane I don't want an abstract husband, I want a real one.

Orgon And what qualities will that real husband have?

Mariane He'll love me.

Orgon That's non-negotiable?

Mariane Ish.
He should be brave. Kind. Strong.

Orgon And wise.

Mariane Okay.

Orgon He must have integrity.

Mariane I think it's best I answer yes to all of these, you're right about most things.

Orgon We agree you should marry a man who possesses these qualities?

Mariane How could I not? You make it sound so obvious, it's what you do, it's your job, you negotiate with businesses and countries and things. You did explain it once but I could never understand it. Mummy always said it was impossible to disagree with you because you always had this way of making everything sound so – well, reasonable and inevitable at the same time.

Orgon Do you trust me, Mariane? That I want the best for you and would never do anything to harm you?

Mariane Yes.

Orgon Good. That's good.
Because I'm going to give you the greatest gift a father can give his daughter.

Mariane Your credit card?

Orgon Your independence.

Mariane My own driver!

Orgon How do I put this? Sooner or later we must all ask ourselves 'What is my legacy?' When I'm gone, what will I leave behind? Will I be remembered as someone who shirked his responsibilities, or a man prepared to take the tough decisions? I won't always be here.

Mariane Daddy!

Orgon And I want to make sure you're taken care of when I'm gone.

Mariane Are you sure you're not dying?

Orgon No, well not immediately, at least not as far as I'm aware.
I want to make sure you're secure. More than secure, comfortable. To pass on all I've worked for. Part of that is wisdom and advice. Part of that – to be blunt – is money.

You're probably aware a sum was due to you when you turn twenty-one, same goes for your brother.

Mariane What do you mean *was* due?

Orgon Well, that's the thing. Circumstances have necessitated a change of time-frame.

Mariane I'm going to have to wait.

Orgon No, no, quite the opposite. I want you to have the money now.

Mariane Really?

Orgon A change in circumstances means it's beneficial to move a substantial sum of money – possibly all of it – from my account into another account – yours for instance – sooner rather than later.

Mariane What change in circumstances?

Orgon Complicated business stuff, nothing to trouble yourself with.
You don't seem pleased.

Mariane No, I am, I'm just a bit taken aback. You've always told me I'm dreadful with money, hopeless at budgeting, and no sooner do I get my allowance than I blow it on absolute nonsense.

Orgon Yes, I did say that.

Mariane And, to be fair, you had a point. But that's going to change. I'm going to change. Thank you for trusting me, Daddy. You're going to see a new me!

Orgon Yes, Mariane, just hold off, you see there is a condition.

Mariane What condition?

Orgon Nothing too, you know . . . Something I think you'd like, something in which you've always expressed an interest.

Mariane Interior design?

Orgon Just – please! In some ways you've grown up too fast, in other ways, not at all. I need to make sure you have someone beside you, in life, who can help you manage that money as well as – well, other areas of your life. Someone to help you make good decisions.

Mariane I'm not very good at that, am I?

Orgon No.

Mariane I don't think things through.

Orgon That's right.

Mariane I take after you in that respect.

Orgon What?

Mariane Mummy was always the sensible one.

Orgon No, she wasn't!

Mariane She was though.

Orgon Look, we're not here to talk about me. We're here to talk about you. And what I'm talking about is a life partner.

Mariane Life partner?

Orgon It's time for you to get married.

Mariane Married? Me? Really?

Orgon Yes.

Mariane What, really really?

Orgon Yes.

Mariane I thought you wouldn't want me to get married.

Orgon Nothing would make me happier.

Mariane I thought you'd say I was way too young.

Orgon Not at all.

Mariane You don't think I'd be rushing in?

Orgon No!

Mariane Well, I do love a party.
Why not?
Let's do it!
I told you you were impetuous!
I'm getting straight on to Feebs at *Tatler*, she is going to *shit*.

She pulls out a phone, starts typing.

And if Arabella thinks she's invited after what she wore at my birthday, she needs to re-evaluate.

Orgon You're not putting this on Facebook, are you?

Mariane Facebook? Seriously? No one's on Facebook any more except for divorcees and paedos.
We need to set a date!

Orgon Sooner the better. We could do it tomorrow?

Mariane Whoa! That's a bit soon. Although that is quite fun. Can you even do that?

Orgon You can in Gibraltar.

Mariane So that's what Gibraltar's for, I always wondered.

Orgon We could fly there – tomorrow!

Mariane This is mad!

Orgon Isn't it?!

Mariane I haven't even asked Valere! What if he's not free, he might have a poetry slam. He'll love it though. Especially when I tell him about the – you know – inheritance. Not that he's into all that. He's a socialist. They don't like money, they're always saying so.

Orgon You're going to tell Valere?

Mariane How else will he know to be there?

Orgon Why does he have to be there?

Mariane Because I'm marrying him.

Orgon You're not marrying Valere.

Mariane Who else would I be marrying?

Orgon We agreed, you need a husband who has integrity, who's wise, financially responsible, Valere is none of those things.

Mariane So who is?

Orgon Tartuffe of course.

Mariane Tartuffe?

Orgon He's perfect for you!

Dorine appears.

Dorine You devious shit.

Orgon Where the hell did you spring from?

Dorine Cleante suspected you were up to something but even I never thought you'd be mad enough to do this!

Orgon I am simply laying down some practical conditions for my daughter's well-being.

Dorine This is how you show your concern, by foisting her on some religious maniac.

Orgon No one is foisting anyone on anyone. Mariane wants to get married.

Dorine Not to Tartuffe.

Orgon All right, let's not get hung up on the small stuff.

Dorine Even if she were to marry, and frankly I don't see the need, why on earth wouldn't she marry Valere?

Orgon He's completely inappropriate.

Dorine Why?

Orgon He's a socialist. And he writes poetry.

Mariane Street poetry.

Dorine Nobody's perfect.

Mariane What's wrong with that?

Orgon Socialism and poetry, they're two of my least favourite things.

Dorine She doesn't want what you want for her, why is that so hard to grasp?

Orgon No, but she needs it.

Dorine Let her be the judge of that.

Orgon This might not seem the ideal match now, but you will grow to love him I promise.

Mariane I'm really not sure I will.

Orgon You're young, you don't have the perspective and wisdom that comes with being middle-aged and giving up on life, love isn't what you think it is.
  Take your late mother and me, we didn't love each other at first but we did all right.

Mariane What do you mean? Of course you and Mummy loved each other?

Orgon We were fond of each other sure, but there was no real spark, we just sort of drunkenly fell into it. You were an accident.

Mariane Oh my God!

Orgon I must have told you this.

Mariane No!

Orgon The point is after six or seven or ten years or so, our affection blossomed into something approximating love.

Mariane I can't believe I'm hearing this.

Orgon Your stepmother on the other hand, that was another story entirely – raw animal lust plus I was probably still grieving for your mother and ultimately this cocktail of booze, grief, and unbridled sexual excess overwhelmed me, I mean we debased ourselves in ways I can scarcely describe.

Mariane Daddy, please.

Orgon At times I barely knew my own name.

Dorine I'm not sure this is helping.

Orgon The point I'm making is passion doesn't last. That's why Tartuffe is a good match, you don't love him, so you'll never be disappointed. That's the secret to a happy marriage – aim low, never be disappointed.

Dorine The words every girl dreams of hearing.

Mariane This is horrible!

Orgon This marriage is the right thing for you!

Dorine For God's sake, tell him how you feel.

Mariane But I can't marry Tartuffe, I can't!

Orgon Why not? Give me one good reason.

Mariane Because I don't want to.

Orgon You don't?

Mariane No.

Orgon Well, why didn't you say?

Mariane I did!

Orgon I didn't know you felt so strongly about it.

Mariane Well, I do.

Orgon And I can't change your mind?

Mariane No.

Orgon Well, I can't force you, can I?

Mariane I just thought you were dead set on it.

Orgon Like I said, you're a young woman now, Mariane, and old enough to make your decisions and I respect that.

Mariane Thank you, Daddy, that means a lot.

Orgon And it also means you're old enough to take responsibility for those decisions. So from now on, you're on your own. As you say, it's time you made your own way in the world, learnt to stand on your own two feet. No more allowance, no more rent-free living, you're out.

Dorine Of the house?

Orgon She wants independence, she can have it and she can say goodbye to any inheritance too.

Dorine You wouldn't.

Orgon I'm doing what I should have done years ago.

Mariane That's not fair.

Orgon I'm asking you to pay your own way, how can that not be fair? I had to, I wasn't born with a silver spoon.

Mariane Things were different then. There were jobs, you could afford to live! What would I do, where would I go, even if I had a job, I can't support myself in this city, no one my age can.

Orgon Then you live under my roof with my rules.
    One last time, before you answer, think carefully – do you object to marrying Tartuffe?

Dorine Oh come on, that's like asking her which hand she'd like you to shit in.

Mariane Daddy, I beg you –

Orgon Do you object?
    I'll take that as a no.

Dorine What would her mother say?

Orgon I am doing this to keep the vow I made to her mother.

Dorine I agree you made mistakes, I agree you were too lax before, but this is too far the other way.

Orgon She needs someone to look after her.

Dorine So does Damis, I don't see you asking him to marry Tartuffe.

Orgon That's different.

Dorine Why?

Orgon Damis isn't into men.

Dorine What he's into's got nothing to do with it, Mariane's not into con men twice her age, that doesn't seem to bother you.

Orgon I don't have to answer to you.

Dorine Will you hear yourself! This is savagery. I'd rather offer myself to Tartuffe than see her consigned to a life of misery.

Orgon As if Tartuffe would be interested in you.

Dorine Why not? You were.

Orgon feigns to slap Dorine. She doesn't flinch.

Go on! If that's who you are now, go on, mark it! Mark what you've become!

Orgon I pay you. Remember that.

Orgon leaves.

Mariane Dorine? Dorine, are you okay? Dorine! Say something!
Dorine, you're starting to freak me out!

Dorine Oh, she speaks! Now she finds her voice!

Mariane Why are you looking at me like that?

Dorine Why didn't you put up a fight?

Mariane I did!

Dorine You call that a fight? I've seen more convincing scraps in the produce aisle in Waitrose.

Mariane What was I supposed to say?

Dorine You're supposed to stand up for yourself!

Mariane When he's like this, he frightens me.

Dorine He would never hurt you.

Mariane He nearly hurt you.
What you said to him –
Dorine, I know we've never spoken about this but I know that after Mummy died, you and Daddy became close.

Dorine You're the priority here, not me. Your father wants to marry you to Tartuffe and we need to work out what to do, that's all that matters right now.

Mariane I already know what I'm going to do.

Dorine You do?

Mariane I've thought it all through. I'm going to kill myself.

Dorine Oh right. I see. It's the killing yourself, is it, uh-huh?

Mariane I've decided it's the only way.

Dorine Well, yeah, it make sense. Have you thought about how you're doing to do it?

Mariane What do you mean?

Dorine Well, you need a method! Wrists in the bath? Bullet to the head? – No, you want a good crowd at the funeral, you'll need an open coffin so nothing too messy. I have it. Drowning. Classic. Everyone loves a drowned woman and water's a terrific metaphor for the untamed mysteries of femininity. Although it does bloat the corpse, so it's six of one, half a dozen of the other.

Mariane I'm serious.

Dorine So am I! Deadly serious. Mariane, killing yourself is no laughing matter, there are down sides. We need a plan, and one that doesn't involve romanticised notions of death.

Mariane You heard Daddy, if I don't marry Tartuffe he'll cut me off.

Dorine You're always telling me you're a feminist.

Mariane I am.

Dorine So what kind of feminism is this? The kind where you only have to stand up for your principles so long as it doesn't impact on your cushy lifestyle?

Mariane Yes, does that kind have a name?

Dorine You know what, I think you should go ahead and marry Tartuffe.

Mariane Oh come on.

Dorine No, no, in fact, the more I think about it, the better suited the both of you are.

Mariane How are Tartuffe and I possibly suited?

Dorine He's just such a fantastic thinker, so full of life. He loves a drink – who doesn't! And going by the amount he eats, I'll bet he has insatiable appetites. Can't imagine a wife of his ever getting bored.

Mariane Dorine!

Dorine You know what a Tartuffe is, by the way? A truffle! And you know what a truffle is – an edible fungal growth. And that's exactly what you'll be popping in your mouth, every weekday night and twice on a Saturday, an edible fungal growth. I'm actually coming round to the idea. If you'll excuse me, I'm off to pick a hat.

Mariane How can you say these things?

Dorine Because you need to understand this is happening.
    No one can force you to marry him, but you have to choose. And that's something you've never had to do – make a real choice, about anything
    There's nothing else for it, you'll just have to get a job.

Mariane Why do you hate me?

Dorine Is it such an awful idea?

Mariane Even if there were any jobs, imagine me working.

I mean it's all right for people like you, Dorine, working types, you're used to jobs, but me.

Dorine Oh darling, you're right, you wouldn't last five minutes, you'd be hopeless. It's not your fault, you've never known any different.

I wouldn't work either if I didn't have to, but I've never had the choice.

Mariane We're so alike you and I, Dorine. Two women bound by the constraints of the patriarchy.

Dorine That's right, love.

Valere enters.

Oh great. Just what we need right now. A poet.

Mariane Valere! You're here. (Are you all right, I think Granny might have seen you jump out of a window?)

Valere I'm not staying.

Mariane You only just got here.

Valere I come only to offer my congratulations.

Mariane For what?

Valere Your imminent marriage.

Dorine Mariane, did you put something online?

Mariane Might have.

Valere So it is true, you are marrying this man Tartuffe!

Mariane Daddy insisted.

Valere You refused, I take it.

Mariane Yes! More or less.

Valere More or less?

Dorine It's complicated.

Valere It's not complicated. 'Do you want to marry Tartuffe?' 'No!' That's literally it.

Mariane He threatened to cut off my money.

Valere Unbelievable. I should have known you weren't committed to the cause.

Mariane No, I am, I really am.

Valere A true socialist would never be swayed by anything so bourgeois as – hang on, what – all your money?

Mariane Yes.

Valere The inheritance and everything?

Mariane He says he's going to throw me out.

Valere Ah. Well that might change things a bit.

Mariane You just said you didn't care about money?

Valere I don't. It just would have been useful for the cause.

Dorine The cause wouldn't be your poetry by any chance, would it?

Valere My politics *is* my art.

Mariane I don't think you even care if I marry Tartuffe.

Valere Well, I shan't influence your decision if that's what you want.

Mariane If that's what you want.

Valere If that's what you want.

Mariane That's what I'm asking you.

Valere Do whatever your heart tells you.

Mariane Maybe it tells me to marry Tartuffe.

Valere In which case I'm sure you'd both be very happy.

Mariane No doubt we would and seeing as you don't even seem to care, I expect you'll have no trouble finding someone to replace me, especially with that pretty little face of yours.

Valere That's actually true, I am awfully pretty.

Mariane You don't love me, I don't love you, you may as well just go.

Valere Then I shall. And good riddance to tainted goods.

Mariane Tainted goods, what do you mean?

Valere You know exactly what I mean!

Mariane I am not and never have been tainted.

Valere I was the one tainted you!

Mariane All we've done is bits.

Valere Oh we've done a lot more than bits.

Mariane You told me that didn't count!

Valere Well it did! Both times!

Mariane And how dare you describe me as *goods*, you're no socialist.

Valere I am too!

Mariane Not in the bedroom, you're not – you're a raging capitalist and so far I am not doing well out of the trickle-down effect.

Valere I believe in an equal redistribution of the orgasm among the sexes, and you know it.

Mariane Your practice lags considerably behind your theory.

Valere How dare you?! I refuse to speak another word to this woman until she apologises.

Mariane Why should I apologise to you? You should be the one who apologises to me!

Valere Then you'll not hear one more word from me.

Mariane Nor you from me.

Valere Suits me fine.

Mariane Still here?

Valere Can't hear you.

Mariane Thought you weren't talking. Dorine, what are you doing?

Dorine I'm just going to lie down here, rest my eyes, let me know when you've finished.

Mariane You're supposed to be helping me.

Dorine I am losing the will to live here, I swear.

Valere All she has to do is tell me she's in the wrong and she won't marry Tartuffe.

Mariane I don't care if I never set eyes on you again as long as I live.

Valere Then consider this the last you'll ever see of me.

Valere exits.

Dorine Okay. What did we learn today?

Mariane Where's he gone?

Dorine You wanted him to go!

Mariane Why would I want him to go?

Valere returns.

Valere Did you say something?

Mariane No, you must have imagined it.

Valere You can't treat me like this, I am a legislator of the human soul!

Valere heads out.

Dorine Give me strength! You! Come back. You! Here, now!

Dorine stops Valere.

Stubborn bloody fools, the pair of you.
   You love her and she loves you, don't throw all that away because of pride.

Valere She doesn't love me.

Mariane And he doesn't love me.

Dorine Enough! God Almighty, you're exhausting me!
   Calm thoughts, calm thoughts.

Mariane None of it matters anyway. The truth is Daddy'll just keep on at me until in the end I give in, like I always do. He's so good at talking me into things, making me think it's what I want and it's only afterwards I realise it wasn't what I wanted at all, it was what he wanted.

Dorine This time it'll be different. This time you'll be strong.

Mariane Maybe he's right, maybe I am stupid and shallow and vain, maybe Tartuffe really is who I need.

Dorine Don't say these things. You're not stupid, you're not – you're not stupid.

Mariane I know I'll give in in the end, it's just a matter of time, I may as well just say yes now.

Dorine Then let's make sure he can't talk you round.

Mariane How?

Dorine What if you married in secret?

Valere Why would she marry Tartuffe in secret? What difference would that make?

Dorine Not Tartuffe, you muppet, you!

Valere Of course, yes! Sorry, I don't follow.

Dorine You said you wanted to get married.

Mariane Yes.

Dorine So marry the right person.
  If you two marry, Mariane couldn't marry Tartuffe even if she wanted to.

Mariane But that'll just make Daddy even more angry.

Dorine We'll deal with that when we come to it. But it gives us time, and hopefully by then your father will have come to his senses.

Valere This is the worse plan I've ever heard.

Dorine Well, let's hear yours, Mr Legislator of the Human Soul.

Mariane He doesn't want to marry me anyway! He doesn't really love me, he never did.

Valere I do love you.

Mariane Then prove it.

Valere I refuse to jump through hoops.

Dorine God alive, just do it, man, before my head explodes.

Valere How can I possibly prove it?

Mariane Compose me a poem.

Valere What, now?

Mariane You're a legislator of the human soul. Well.
Legislate.

Valere I can't just do it to order.
    I need time and solitude, the muse to strike.

Dorine If the prospect of the woman you love, who loves
you, marrying another man, doesn't stoke the fires of
creativity, then you're not a poet, you're a hack.

Valere Very well. A poem.
    I'm calling this one . . . 'Mind Control' . . .

    Ahmed and Ollie work the nine-to-five but the boss man
    he don't care about no living wage
    'cause the mainstream media poisoned his mind
    now the government's on his back.

Dorine Christ Almighty, what is that?

Valere It's a truth bomb.

    Rewind.

It's a truth bomb straight from the front line of the war
on consciousness exploding live and direct into your
brain.

Mariane I don't want a truth bomb, I want a nice poem.

Valere Nice? Nice?!

Mariane Yes, and I want it to rhyme.

Valere You want it to *what*?

Mariane Rhyme.

Valere You know full well I don't do ones that rhyme.

Dorine What kind of poet can't rhyme?

Valere I can rhyme, it is a political choice. Rhyme is a bourgeois construct that serves to constrain language in a penitentiary of form – a desperate attempt by the powers-that-be to create the illusion of order in a world governed by the fascist conspiracy that seeks to oppress the workers.

Mariane If it doesn't rhyme I don't want it.

Valere Why does no one respect the revolution?!
All right! I'll do it.
Ridiculous.

Valere composes in his head, rejecting certain combinations, counting off syllables on his fingers.

Dorine In your own time.

Valere I have a process.
I'm counting the syllables.

Mariane, Mariane
Mariane
Mariane
Let me be your man
For who else loves you the way I . . . do
And though it would be easy to misconstrue
The depth of feeling I have for you
I assure you, my love, that my love is true.

Mariane, I offer you the poetry of true feeling, simply expressed.
I love you with my heart and soul.
We don't need money. We have each other. If needs be, we can move to the country, start a commune and live off the land, humble but happy. I shall write poetry and you shall milk cows.
Let me be your husband.
What do you say?
Will you be my wife?

47

Mariane No.

I won't be anyone's wife. Unless it's my choice and this is no choice at all.

I'll be your lover, your friend, but I won't be constrained by a ring, any more than you would be by language.

Valere Is this a test?

Mariane It's not a test. Sometimes, you have to stand up for yourself.

Valere You want me to prove myself!

Mariane No, no, Valere, that's not what I'm –

Valere And like the poet-pugilist I am, I shall prove myself not just with the flick-knife of language, but with action. And like the great lovers of history – Casanova, Don Juan, Russell Brand (before he settled down) – I shall earn your love.

Mariane That's not how it works.

Valere Hush! Not another word. Next time you see me, it will be as your liberator.

Valere leaves through a door.

Mariane Isn't that the room where you keep the cleaning things?

Dorine nods.
Valere returns through the same door.
Valere leaves through a different door.

Mariane Daddy's right. It's time I grew up.

Mariane leaves.

Dorine

You have to give it to her though, she's right –
Not much of a wedding night,

48

Is it, with a man you hardly know,
Let alone like or love? No,
Forced love is no love at all,
So fair play to the girl for standing tall.
As for Orgon, he's lost to reason, that much is clear –
An idea! I think it's time for a word with Elmire.

Three

Dorine makes sure the room is fit for purpose – for Elmire, as we will discover.
Enter Damis.

Damis Where is he?

Dorine I didn't hear you come in!

Damis Where is that coward Tartuffe!

Dorine Will you lower your voice?

Damis Have you heard what he's trying to do? He's wormed his way into Pa's head and now Pa's trying to force Mariane to marry Tartuffe.

Dorine Yes, I have. Look, Tartuffe'll be down any second and your stepmother is going to try and convince him not to do that, but she needs privacy –

Damis It just makes me angry, you know, the idea that there are men like Tartuffe who don't see women as autonomous human beings with their own thoughts, their own desires, their own dreams of a better, more just, more fem-centric world, well, it's men like that who give allies like me a bad name –

Dorine That's nice, Damis, but I really need you to leave.

Damis If more men just listened to women, none of this would be a problem, that's the new model for a strong man, you have to listen to the women. Listen to the women. You have to listen to the women.

Sorry, what were you saying?

Dorine I need you to leave.

Damis Leave? I can't leave. I have to stop Tartuffe bullying my sister into marrying him.

Dorine Damis, we already have a plan.

Damis Great, what is it!

Dorine I just told you!

Damis Did you? Sorry, I wasn't listening.

Dorine There's no time now, I just need you to leave.

Damis No, no, no, if there's a plan, I need to be a part of it, as the man of the house, all plans have to be approved by me.

Dorine Why?

Damis That's just rules, isn't it?

Dorine Since when are you even the man of the house?

Damis Since Pa went bonkers.

Dorine peeks out of the door.

Dorine He's coming! Damis, please.

Damis If something's going down, I need to be here!

Dorine No!

Damis hides.
Tartuffe enters, with a towel of large cloth.
He locates a bucket and ice dispenser in a drinks cabinet – fills the bucket with ice and washes himself ritually.

Tartuffe May the God of the heavens and the earth preserve, sanctify, purge us of excess, make our true selves known to all.

Tartuffe dries himself.

Oh hello. I didn't see you there, I was caught up in the spirit, *namaste*.

Dorine I was hoping to see you actually.

Tartuffe You've not been waiting for me, I hope?
Were you expecting me sooner? – I tend to rise late.

Dorine I had noticed.

Tartuffe Mornings are when I like to nourish the self in order that in the afternoon I may nourish others.

Dorine What a charming image.

He offers Dorine the bucket.

No, I won't, I'm trying not to.
Something I can help you with?

Tartuffe Does it bother you, me looking at you?

Dorine It is a little unsettling I have to say.

Tartuffe If you don't want to be looked at, you should consider how you dress, you'll give a man ideas with that neckline.

Dorine Well, you could always look somewhere else.

Tartuffe Why show the man the buffet if he's not invited to eat?

Dorine I could come up with something witty building on the food metaphor but how about just fuck off?
Funny how the merest glimpse of skin is enough to send you into a frenzy, but the thought of you naked does nothing for me.

Tartuffe Interesting.

Dorine Why is that interesting?

Tartuffe No, it's just interesting that you would talk about me being naked – is it something you've thought about? I'm not trying to put words in your mouth, I'm just curious.

Dorine Mm, you are curious.

Tartuffe People tell me I'm a very perceptive person.

Dorine Do they?

Tartuffe They do, and you strike me as a closed person, a closed and angry person. Sometimes the Lord talks to me, gives me little words and insights and I get a strong sense of anger and closed-offness from you, I'm getting the image of a flower that hasn't been pollinated, does that mean anything to you, I'm not judging, it's just an observation, I'm just reflecting it back, maybe let it sit with you awhile, see if it stirs anything.

Anyway, I've enjoyed this little whatever it is but I'm afraid I have more pressing matters to –

Dorine Elmire would like to see you. In private.

Tartuffe Elmire?

Dorine Yes.

Tartuffe Here?

Dorine Yes.

Tartuffe Now?

Dorine Yes. But if you're busy I'll –

Tartuffe If the lady of the house wishes to see me, who am I to say no?

Dorine Who are you indeed?

Tartuffe Have I upset you in some way?

Dorine I don't like what you've done to this family.

Tartuffe What's the harm in a little disruption? It's healthy. Reminds us it's all on loan.

Dorine What is?

Tartuffe This. All of it. This house, this room. (This rather enormous room?)
 Orgon, who I think employs you, invited me here, if he asks me to leave I'll go.
 He seems to think I have something to offer.
 Perhaps there's something I can offer you.

Dorine I've met your sort.
 Full of ideas, hanging around wealthy people, claiming you want to overturn the old order, that you're in it, but somehow not of it. But all the while you drink the wine, eat the food, stain the sheets. You like the spoils as much as the next man. Know what you really are? A plain old social climber, you just won't admit it.

Tartuffe Takes one to know one.

Dorine I don't claim to be anything I'm not.

Tartuffe What happened, after their mother died, thought you'd just slot in, change of role? Then in waltzes Elmire? Charm, beauty, grace, none of it earned. Effortless. And you so loyal.
 Namaste.

Dorine Elmire will be down shortly. I'll let her know you're ready to receive her.

Tartuffe Always.

 Exit Dorine.
  Tartuffe offers a prayer.
  He needs something. The bucket.
  He puts the bucket on a waist-high surface.
  He checks to see if anyone is watching.
  He dunks his person into the bucket of ice water.

Tartuffe removes himself, dries himself briskly with the towel.
Enter Elmire.

Elmire Is this a bad time?

Tartuffe No! A simple cleansing ritual.
Namaste.

Elmire Oh yes, *namaste.*

Tartuffe Are you recovered? Your fever.

Elmire Passed.

Tartuffe My intercession was not in vain.

Elmire There's really no need to trouble the Lord on my behalf, I'm sure he has so much on.

Tartuffe He cares for all his children. Especially those with such beauty.

Elmire I had no idea he was so focused on outward appearance?

Tartuffe I was referring to your inner light.

Elmire Of course you were. I was hoping we might have a little chat.

Tartuffe Nothing would give me greater pleasure – well, almost nothing.

Elmire It's quite difficult to talk with you all the way over there.

Tartuffe I should come closer?

Elmire It would help, yes.
You can come closer than that.
Maybe not quite that close.

Tartuffe Forgive me, I'm afflicted by a surfeit of zeal.

Elmire Shall we sit?

Tartuffe I'd rather stand.

Elmire Do I make you uncomfortable in some way?

Tartuffe I was about to ask you the same question.
I can't help wondering if your fever was merely a pretext on which to avoid me.

Elmire Why would I avoid you?

Tartuffe I have been known to arouse strong feelings in a certain type of woman.

Elmire And which type is that?

Tartuffe The neglected type.

Elmire I was under the impression you didn't like me.

Tartuffe Nothing could be further from the truth.

Elmire Banning me from having visitors in my own house, slandering my character with unfounded and malicious gossip to all and sundry, it conveys an impression.

Tartuffe If I raise objections to your choice of companions, it's to protect your reputation.

Elmire Why such concern with reputation if it's one's inner beauty that counts?

Tartuffe We cannot choose the times in which we live. Sadly we are judged by how things appear.

Elmire Your hand.

Tartuffe What of it?

Elmire It has a mind of its own.

Tartuffe Forgive me, I was distracted.

Elmire By what?

Tartuffe Your fur.
    The lining, is it real?

Elmire Faux, I'm afraid. I can't abide unnecessary cruelty.

Tartuffe Is there any other kind?

Elmire My husband doesn't know I'm talking to you.

Tartuffe Interesting.

Elmire There's an issue I was hoping we might resolve with some discretion.

Tartuffe You have my word.

Elmire My husband wants you and Mariane to marry. It's a little much, wouldn't you say? Leaving aside the small matter of whether she even likes you, a wife is, after all, for life not just for Christmas.

Tartuffe I believe you're overlooking the spiritual and physical dimensions. And one should never overlook the dimensions.

Elmire I'm a pragmatist. I have little time for ideology of any stripe, I like things I can see, I prefer to get things done.
    My husband feels you offer him something.

Tartuffe He offers me things too.

Elmire I'm sure he does. He has it in his head you should marry Mariane, which some might consider a little . . .

Tartuffe Old-fashioned?

Elmire I was going to say reactionary but *you do you*. The point is I'm pretty sure it's not what Mariane wants.

Tartuffe Without her consent it can't happen.

Elmire But I'm worried in the attempt to persuade her, Orgon may create well – unpleasantness.

Tartuffe And we don't want unpleasantness, do we?

Elmire No. We don't.
How do you feel about this proposed marriage?

Tartuffe As I say, uneasy.

Elmire Good.

Tartuffe It's not the match I had in mind, you see.

Elmire And what did you have in mind?

Tartuffe A greater prize.

Elmire Ah. I see. How flattering
Prize is an interesting choice of word. Sort of implies something you get rather than something you do.
In any case, shouldn't a man like you have eyes only for Heaven?

Tartuffe I'm certainly not above casting my gaze a little lower.
There is after all only so long a man may stare at the sun before he goes blind.

Elmire Or mad.

Tartuffe I can bear this no longer.

Elmire Bear what?

Tartuffe What you do to me!

Elmire I'm not doing anything to you.

Tartuffe My life's journey has been one of self-realisation and acceptance, understanding who I am – may I speak directly?

Elmire As long as you promise not to use the word 'journey'.

Tartuffe But in your presence, all that work is undone, my senses overwhelmed with such intensity of feeling.

As I look at you now, I feel God's presence stirring within me.

Elmire Let me get that bucket.

Tartuffe At first I thought you were sent by the devil himself to tempt me.

Elmire You thought what?

Tartuffe I resolved to appal you, drive you away.

Elmire You certainly did that.

Tartuffe But I kept being drawn back like a moth to a flame.

I thought you were an obstacle to my salvation, but then like a bolt from above it hit me.

Elmire Please, vulgarity I can abide, but not cliché.

Tartuffe You were not the obstacle to salvation. You are my salvation! You're not undoing the Lord's work, you're fulfilling it!

I thought the Lord had sent me here to save you all.

I had it the wrong way round.

He sent me here so you could save me!

Elmire I think there's been some crossed wires between you and the Lord.

Tartuffe I abandon myself to your mercy. My hope I place in your goodness, my heart I place in your hands –

Elmire I'm going to have to stop you before you think of anything else you want to place somewhere.

Tartuffe God reveals himself through his creation. And what greater evidence of his perfection than you.

Elmire I thought you were a holy man.

Tartuffe Holy, yes, but a man also! As you are a woman.

Elmire A married woman and I'm pretty sure *He* or *She* or whoever's bloody up there has something to say about that.

Tartuffe God lives in me. And if God is holy, it follows that anything within me is of God, for in God sin itself is sanctified, do you see?

Elmire Sorry, I'm going to have to ask, what the fuck are you talking about?

Tartuffe One word from you will make or break me, my happiness resides in your arms.

Elmire That's a responsibility too far.

Tartuffe Who am I, a mere instrument of the Lord, to deny that which God himself has placed in my heart.

Elmire He hasn't placed it in mine.

Tartuffe If you condemn my feelings, you condemn their author, that is the true blasphemy.

Elmire What are you doing?

Tartuffe As the good book says, let not the right hand know what the left is up to.

Elmire You're supposed to be my husband's mentor or his guide or his friend or something.

Tartuffe I would never break the holy bond of confession.

Elmire What the hell does that mean?

Tartuffe I can be very discreet.

Elmire Stop, stop, stop.
  Take your bloody hands off me. None of this is okay, none of it, what do you think this is, the nineties?

Tartuffe Forgive me. I am flesh and blood, I'm so ashamed!
   I am a worm!

Elmire Will you stop this worm business, I'm already struggling under the weight of all this metaphor.

Tartuffe You must understand how much I respect you as a human being; and also as a woman.

Elmire As a human being and a woman I'm thrilled to hear that.

Tartuffe My behaviour is unforgivable, I have shamed myself, forgive me! You must tell your husband the kind of man I am.

Elmire All right, all right, enough of the self-flagellation.
   There's no need to tell my husband about this.
   I'm sure we can come to some sort of arrangement.

Tartuffe What kind of arrangement?

Elmire We'll keep this whatever it was to ourselves on one condition.

Tartuffe Name it.

Elmire It's about Mariane.

   Damis appears.

Damis So this is your so called plan!

Elmire God alive, Damis.

Damis I knew there was something funny going on.

Elmire How long have you been there?

Damis Long enough to uncover your betrayal!

Elmire What betrayal?

Damis I heard everything! Well, nearly everything, the sound's a bit muffled in there, but I heard enough about your 'arrangement' to know exactly what's going on.

Elmire No, no, no, Damis, you misunderstand, I was right on the verge of something.

Damis I know exactly what you were on the verge of!

Elmire You've got this all wrong!

Damis I'm going to tell Pa what I've seen.

Elmire No, no, Damis.

Damis He's going to be so proud of me!

Orgon enters.

Orgon What the hell is this?

Damis Yes! Yes! Right on cue!
    Father, I have a tale to astonish you. Your loyalty, your generosity, hospitality, this gentleman has thrown them all in your face. This fiend has led you by the nose for too long, and I am the one to unmask him.

Elmire Damis, I know you think you're helping but you're not.

Damis It would suit my stepmother to keep you in the dark, but I cannot be party to a lie.

Orgon What lie?

Elmire This is all a misunderstanding.

Damis I interrupted your man Tartuffe on the brink of making love to your wife.

Orgon Is this true?

Elmire No!

Tartuffe Yes, it's true, it's all true!

Damis See how he denies it!

   Oh hang on, he's not denying it. Right. Hadn't really planned for that.

Tartuffe Your son is right, I'm a sinner, and a scoundrel. A fake and a fraud, the most heinous hypocrite ever walked the earth. Your fury is justified. I have offended Heaven and you. Hound me from your home, hurl me to the gutter. No shame is too great, no punishment too severe, I am not who you think I am, I have deceived you!

Damis That was easy. Well done me.

   Orgon is looking at Tartuffe.

Orgon How could you betray me like this?

   Damis triumphant.

(*To Damis.*) My own son! How dare you try and sully this man's good name?

Damis Me? *I've* betrayed you?

Orgon Maligning the character of my friend!

Tartuffe But he's right!

Orgon Don't believe their lies.

Tartuffe He's telling the truth!

Orgon I know what you're trying to do.

Tartuffe You do?

Orgon You're a good man.

Tartuffe I am?

Orgon They're jealous of your nobility, your meekness.

Tartuffe They are?

Orgon You want to protect them but you mustn't.

Elmire Have you lost your mind?

Orgon Damis, you should be ashamed.

Damis But he admits it!

Tartuffe And that's the least of it! I'm a hypocrite, a murderer, a thief, and a fraud, there's not a name yet invented I don't deserve to be called!

Heap shame on me, I welcome your condemnation, I beg you for it!

Orgon Hear how penitent he is.

Damis He's playing you for a fool.

Orgon I won't hear another word.

Damis The man's a liar and a cheat.

Orgon Quiet or I'll break your fucking arms.

Elmire Orgon!

Tartuffe Show him mercy, he's just a boy! Look upon him, the openness in his face, the strength in his heart, the hope in his eyes, the bloom of youth upon him. Look! Look! and tell me – is this the face of evil?

Orgon See how he defends you, even as you condemn him.

Elmire You're not falling for this cabaret?

Orgon You're trying to turn me against him, the pair of you.

Damis We're protecting you from yourself.

Orgon The more you try and get rid of him, the more I shall embrace him.

Tartuffe will marry your sister.

And if she doesn't like that, she can try her luck in the gutter. You want to live under my roof, you live by my rules, this disobedience stops now!

And how dare you accuse him of treachery.
How dare you?
Beg him for forgiveness.

Damis I've done nothing wrong.

Orgon Beg him!

Damis I refuse.

Orgon Then this house is no longer your house. Leave and never return.

Elmire He's your son.

Orgon I have no son.

Damis exits.

Elmire If there is a God, may She forgive you what you've done.

Elmire exits.

Orgon What have I done? What have I done? I spoke in anger, I was too harsh.

Tartuffe Wait!
The worst is over, you've been though the storm, the wind has abated, don't weaken now, harden your resolve.

Orgon Yes! Yes! You're right, you're always right.

Tartuffe I am.
But now I must go. I must leave this house and not return.

Orgon Leave? You can't leave.

Tartuffe I have brought trouble to your home.

Orgon You can't go, without you I'm nothing.

Tartuffe I've divided your family.

Orgon Better division than sin.

Tartuffe The stories they tell about me will become worse. The lies more extreme.

Orgon The righteous are always persecuted.

Tartuffe Next time you may believe them.

Orgon No.

Tartuffe They'll take advantage of your trusting nature.

Orgon I won't allow it.

Tartuffe You say that now, there will come a time when you doubt me.

Orgon I will remain strong.

Tartuffe It's the only way, I must go.

Orgon Please, Tartuffe, don't leave me.
  I beg you!
  I couldn't live without you.

Tartuffe As you wish.
  But I must keep some distance between myself and your wife or the gossips will have a field day.

Orgon Let them.
  Let's confound them.

Tartuffe How?

Orgon Let them see you with her all the time, see what they make of that.

Tartuffe Are you sure?

Orgon Rub their noses in your purity, expose the filth in their minds for what it is.
  Morning, noon and night, you must spend as much time as possible alone with my wife.

Tartuffe Morning, noon and night. Are you sure?

Orgon I've never been more certain.

Tartuffe Alone.

Orgon Let's really give them something to talk about. It'll be our joke. Our secret.

Tartuffe Okay.

Orgon It's rare for a man to meet so trusted a friend. That very first moment I laid eyes on you, I knew I'd met someone who –
  I've not known companionship like this since my days in service.

Tartuffe Adversity strengthens all bonds between men.

Orgon They told me you're eating and drinking too much.

Tartuffe When they stop, I will stop.
  To heal the world, you must love the world. To love the world you must know the world. To know the world you must become as the world is. I must refine myself in the fire of earthly need, face the enemy head on. Only then can people be saved.

Orgon You put yourself through so much. Who's going to look after you?
  If anything should happen –
  I want you to be a part of me – my family.
  As one leaves, so another takes his place.
  You and Mariane will marry.

Tartuffe I'll marry Mariane?

Orgon Yes, you'll marry.

Tartuffe Mariane?

Orgon Yes.

Tartuffe I'm not sure she's keen.

Orgon Mariane?

Tartuffe No.

Orgon She'll come round, I'll make sure.
There are things closer than blood. I'll have the contract drawn up. Make it official.

Tartuffe As you wish.

Orgon You'd look after her, wouldn't you? You'd be good to her.

Tartuffe I'd treat her like my own daughter.
Something weighing on you?

Orgon I don't know who else to tell.
In the last rather ill-advised war, I served with some distinction. Marked myself out as a man to be counted on. It's how I came by my title and all that entails. When I retired from service, our leaders continued to regard me as a safe pair of hands.
So during the recent upheavals, I was entrusted with a degree of knowledge, which I employed to my advantage, speculating on certain investments, some of which were perhaps contrary to the nation's interests.
I did rather well out of it. *Very* well, in fact. I mean it's really something, all you need is a few hours' head start on the markets and the numbers are – sorry, I'm –

Tartuffe But isn't what you're talking about quite –

Orgon Yes. It is quite. Very quite.
It's – well, more excitable factions might even call it – Treason.
While I was *in the country* it became clear that due to the current climate some of these indiscretions might be disclosed, certain documents brought to light
You can't begin to understand, the shame so heavy on my conscience.

68

I can't eat or sleep. It's driving me mad.

It's exactly as you said, that first day we met. This is my reckoning.

Tell me what to do. Help me!

Tartuffe A full confession must be made.

Orgon Of course. I will make representations to the authorities first thing.

Tartuffe The authorities? This is no matter for the authorities.

Orgon But I thought –

Tartuffe What you describe is far too grave to be handed over to some mere human court, this concerns your soul.

Orgon My soul?

Tartuffe Orgon, I will receive your confession. But you must tell me everything.

Orgon Everything.

Tartuffe Stint on nothing. Every last detail. In writing. It's the only way.

Orgon My one true friend.

Tartuffe And I should probably take a look at any documents you have hanging around.

But first we must pray.

Orgon
What to say, where to start?

Tartuffe
Just tell me what's on your heart,
The truth will set you free.

Orgon
You promise?

Tartuffe
You don't trust me?

Orgon
Of course, I'm just scared that's all.

Tartuffe
Your fears are perfectly natural
But they must be overcome.

Orgon
You're right. You're so like a . . .

Tartuffe
Son?

Orgon
Yes. How I can ever possibly repay –?

Tartuffe
Oh I'm sure we'll find a way
Now –

Orgon
Oh yes.

Tartuffe
Namaste.

Tartuffe acknowledges the audience, as Orgon continues to pray.

Four

Tartuffe.
* With him, an acolyte – similar attire. Not identical.*
More a variation on a clear theme.
* One or two more join during the scene, quietly*
working or praying.
* Cleante enters.*

Cleante *Namaste.*

Tartuffe *Namaste.*
  I was at prayer.

Cleante I saw.

* Cleante picks up one of Tartuffe's cards.*

'Truth, friend'.
  What is that?

Tartuffe There's no mystery. It means I am here to bring
truth. Friend.

Cleante Thank you. Friend.
  Strange thing, friendship. You meet someone as a
young man, spend your whole life looking up to them,
admiring them. They're there for you, through everything.
Life, death, marriage, divorce. Your rock. The person you
go to when life is tricky. Then one day it turns out, they
need you more than you need them.
  To watch them throw their life away on a ten-a-penny
charlatan and know there's not a damn thing you can
do about it, well that's funny, right? So why am I not
laughing?

Tartuffe You're here to tell me to leave your friend alone, I admire that.

Cleante No, no. I have to accept that Orgon's in thrall. I watched the same thing happen with him and my sister, it's a trait.

Tartuffe I think you underestimate your sister.

Cleante I never underestimate my sister. Nor should you.
    No, Orgon's a big boy, whatever he does to himself, that's on him, I'm here because of his children.
    Orgon is one thing, but his kids? That's not the behaviour of an honourable man. It's base. It's low.

Tartuffe I'm not going after anyone, it was Damis who went after me.

Cleante He was defending his sister.

Tartuffe That's interesting, I thought he was defending his inheritance.

Cleante He's been thrown out of his own home.

Tartuffe I know, isn't it awful?

Cleante It happened because of you!

Tartuffe It happened because of his pride. It breaks my heart to see the poor boy suffering.

Cleante Then speak to Orgon, get him to change his mind, he listens to you.

Tartuffe I did speak to him. I pleaded with him. My only regret is he ignored my counsel.

Cleante It doesn't trouble you, the inheritance due to Damis is now going to you?

Tartuffe Not me, my work.

Cleante The distinction eludes me.

Tartuffe What exercises you? That Orgon won't give his money to his son, or that I'm the beneficiary? What's it to you, on whom Orgon chooses to bestow his fortune?

Cleante Damis is my sister's stepson.

Tartuffe Ah! So it's the fact he's one of your own, rather than any injustice that exercises you?

Cleante Can't it be both?

Tartuffe You don't like me because I'm not one of you, I'm an outsider.

Cleante I don't like you because you're an imposter and you're ruining the lives of my sister's family.

Tartuffe How am I an imposter? I'm not pretending to be anything other than that which I am.

Cleante And what is that?

Tartuffe A friend. To Orgon. One who loves him enough to tell him uncomfortable truths about his own family.

Cleante What right have you to take what belongs to Damis?

Tartuffe What Orgon does with his money is his concern.

Cleante A father's money should pass to his children, that is right and just.

Tartuffe Just that wealth is acquired by an accident of birth?

Cleante Oh I see, you're ushering in the revolution.

Tartuffe A boy can dream.

Cleante God dammit, you're slippery.
  I'm having a drink. You joining me? I know you like a drink.

Tartuffe If it pleases you, I'll join you, sure.

Cleante What do you want?

Tartuffe Same as you.

Cleante No – what do you want?
That's what I'm asking.

Tartuffe And I'm telling you I want the same as you.
Same thing all of us want.

Cleante And what is that?

Tartuffe The truth, / friend.

Cleante overlaps at the slash.

Cleante Friend. This faith of yours, it's not strictly
Judaeo-Christian, you're not a Buddhist, what is it, seems
like more of a mish-mash, almost as if you're grabbing
anything to hand.

Tartuffe Traditions are merely spokes of the same wheel.

Cleante And in which direction is this wheel of yours
turning?

Tartuffe Towards truth, brother. Always truth. The
people are hungry for it.

Cleante Either that or so starved they'll swallow any old
bullshit.
You know when you turned up I had you down as a
straight-up con man, now I'm not sure.
You're clever, but that doesn't explain it. Not much to
look at, no discernible charisma and your personal hygiene
is questionable.

Tartuffe Thank you.

Cleante So what's the appeal?
Orgon talks about your eyes, the lustre, but when I look
at them I just see pools of black.
What kind of name is Tartuffe anyway?
Is that even your real name?

74

Tartuffe Is any of this real?

Cleante Oh come on! Seriously!
  Oh my God. You actually believe it. That's it. That's the trick. You really believe it, at least when you say it you do.

Tartuffe You'd like to think of me as a con man, wouldn't you, that would reassure you, you'd be able to place me, you'd feel secure in the knowledge there's nothing you're missing. But the idea I might be the real thing, that scares you, doesn't it? Threatens your sense of the world.

Cleante You don't scare me.

Tartuffe Then why are you trembling?

Cleante Some sort of chill in the air.

Tartuffe Interesting.
  What is it you do exactly?

Cleante Do?

Tartuffe For work. Do you work?

Cleante These days I mostly sit on a few boards. Charities, galleries, theatres.

Tartuffe One of those people with your name on a chair?

Cleante Yeah, that's me.

Tartuffe Giving something back.

Cleante I'm a fully paid-up hateful liberal with hypocrisy coming out of my ears, you're on to nothing new there, pal. But for what it's worth, I do actually think I'm doing something useful, something of value.
  I mean you laugh at the idea of giving something back, what am I supposed to do, keep it all?

Tartuffe You say when you look into my eyes, all you see is black. Maybe that's your own emptiness reflected back, maybe that's why Orgon sees something lustrous – because his heart is full of light.

You have no idea the depth of your hypocrisy.

You think it's just the trappings.

Everything you're built upon is corrupt.

When I look at you, beneath the nothing-fazes-me façade, you know what I see?

The acolytes have stopped and are watching.

Cleante What's that?

Tartuffe Terror.

Cleante Is that so?

Tartuffe Yes.

The foundations are shaking.

This is all coming down.

With you inside.

I say that in love.

Cleante Neat little parlour trick you have there.

Tartuffe *Namaste*, friend.

Tartuffe exits.
  Cleante alone.
  Dorine, Mariane and Elmire appear.

Elmire Out! Out!

The acolytes disperse.

It's an infestation, that bloody man's taking over.

Any joy?

Cleante Nothing. I got to say, he nearly managed to get under my skin, it's interesting, he's really quite something.

Elmire What is wrong with you?

Cleante Nothing's wrong with me, I'm just saying he has some interesting ideas.

Dorine Elmire, you need to talk to Orgon about Mariane.

Elmire Why don't you talk to him?

Dorine He won't listen to me.

Elmire You think he'll listen to me? You saw what happened with Damis.

Dorine We have to do something.

Cleante We need to appeal to his emotions, he's beyond reason.

Dorine Then it has to be Mariane.

Mariane Me?

Elmire She's right. If he'll listen to anyone, it's you.

Mariane But you saw what he was like before –

Elmire He loves you. Use that. Fathers are weird about their daughters – trust me, they just are – if anyone can get to him, it's you.

Dorine Lay it on thick.

Mariane Right.

Elmire Not too thick or he'll suspect.

Mariane Okay.

Cleante Flatter him.

Dorine But don't pander to him.

Mariane Right.

Cleante Speak from the heart to the heart.

Mariane Thick but not too thick, flatter but don't pander, from the heart to the heart.

Elmire Perfect.

Mariane Yes.
What was the first one again?

Enter Orgon.

Oh God, I can't do this.

Dorine Think of what's at stake, this is your future.

Orgon I see. The committee's here.

Mariane Daddy, please don't make me marry a man
I don't love.

Dorine The direct approach, I like it.

Orgon You may not thank me now, but I promise you,
one day you will.

Mariane I know why you're doing this. You weren't
there for me when Mummy died and now you want to
make amends.

Orgon My mind is made up.

Mariane I'm a disappointment to you, it's true.

Orgon You could never be a disappointment.

Mariane Please, Daddy, I may be stupid but I'm not an
idiot.
You think I'm vain and conceited and selfish and
spoilt, it's true, don't try and deny it, but if I am, it's
because you made me this way.
You never taught me to stand on my own feet and now
you blame me when I can't. You infantilised me from the
word go, Daddy's little girl – and guess what, I'm an
infant.

Orgon So it's my fault?

Mariane You loved the idea of being the provider, the
great myth of how you pulled yourself up by your own

bootstraps, no help from anyone – oh no, my children don't have to work!

Orgon I wanted a better life for you than the one I had.

Mariane You wanted us to be dependent on you so you could lord it over us with tales of how you did this all yourself!

Orgon You think it was easy, the sacrifices I made?

Mariane I never said it was easy but it was possible. In the world you grew up in. It's not the same now. Roll your eyes all you like, but this is your doing. Sat on your pot of money, doling it out on a whim, acting like it's generosity when it's not, it's about control.

Orgon How can you be so ungrateful, you never wanted for anything?

Mariane You're supposed to teach me the value of things, you're my parent, that's your job.

Dorine She's right, you know she is.

Orgon What do you think I'm doing now?

Mariane This isn't about me, this is about your guilt.
    And you know what, maybe it is my fault. Maybe I do need to be taught a lesson but not like this.
    Don't make me choose between sharing a bed with a man I despise and being forced from your house, because I will leave.
    You talk about the cost to me, well the cost to you if I walk out that door is you will never see me again, your own daughter.

Dorine Isn't she doing well?

Mariane Is that what you want?
    You're not a monster, Daddy. You used to tell me when you looked at me I reminded you of Mummy.

79

Dorine Yes!

Cleante Quiet!

Mariane What would Mummy say to you now?
    I don't want your money, just for you to acknowledge me as a woman with desires and dreams of my own, however silly you think they are, they're mine. They're who I am.

Orgon Stay strong, Orgon, you must stay strong, hold fast to the truth!

Mariane Because if you force me on to the streets, you leave me no choice but to contemplate the most extreme course of action available.

Orgon Oh God, Mariane, you can't possibly mean –

Mariane Yes.
    I'll have no other choice but to join *Médecins Sans Frontières*.

Orgon Join what?

Mariane *Médecins Sans Frontières*. It's a charity, they provide aid to war zones.

Orgon Yeah, I know what it is, I just don't know why you're talking about it.

Mariane Because I'll run away and join them.

Orgon Run away and join them? It's an aid organisation, not the fucking circus.

Mariane Why are you all looking at me like that?

Dorine You were doing so well, Mariane.

Cleante *Médecins Sans Frontières*, really?

Mariane What?

Orgon Right up until then, I thought you were serious.

Mariane I am serious, I'm going to devote my life to service.

Orgon Do you even know what it involves?

Mariane Yes. You hand over packages of food to children with dirty little faces, I've seen it on YouTube, they're ever so grateful.

Orgon Enough! This ends here. You marry Tartuffe – tomorrow.

Cleante That's quite short notice.

Mariane Apparently you can do it in Gibraltar.

Dorine So that's what Gibraltar's for.

Orgon Make your choice, Mariane.
   Are you staying or going? And remember if you leave and I never see you again, that's your decision, not mine.
   I won't be ignored in this, I will be obeyed.
   Or mark my words, you'll get nothing, nothing!

Mariane I never could argue with you.
   Fine. You win. Have it your way.
   Nothing.
   I choose nothing.
   What else can I do?
   But I will always miss you. And I will always love you, Daddy, always. No matter what.

Cleante Look me in the eye, tell me you're not moved.

Orgon I have to be strong! I have to be strong!

Elmire You ridiculous man! Are you so arrogant you won't listen to your own daughter? What does your heart tell?

Orgon The heart is full of deceit.

Elmire Trust yourself!

Orgon No. No! This rebellion ends now. You will not talk me out of this.

I am the head of this household, no one else.

Elmire Head of the household, you're not even master of your own will.

First me, then your son, now your daughter – everyone who cares about you, you push away.

Orgon I told you, I don't have a son.

Elmire You don't get to choose that.

Orgon The venomous lies he spoke about Tartuffe –

Elmire He was trying to show you who he really is.

Orgon You wanted Tartuffe to seduce you, that's why you concocted this vain fantasy about him being besotted with you!

Elmire That's your opinion of me?

Orgon You hardly looked distraught at the proposition.

Elmire If I shouted the house down every time some pillock with roving hands made an unwelcome advance I'd be hoarse within a week.

You have no idea, do you? Subjected to your gaze, your whims, your feckless vanity, the endless negotiations we make so as not to offend your fragile little egos, it's like calculus, and stupidly, stupidly I expected more from you.

You're tearing your family apart and for what? Pride? What is this hold he has on you?

Orgon Before him nothing made sense, now it does, he changed my life, he can do the same for Mariane, she can't see it yet, because she's blind, but he will open her eyes, and he will open yours too if you put aside your arrogance.

Elmire You don't even care if she marries him, do you?

82

Orgon I cannot force her.

Elmire This was never about her, this is about you.
You're not trying to marry her off, you're trying to marry him in. This is a way to keep him close to you. My God, you're in love and you'd do anything to show him the depths of that love, even hand him your own daughter.

Orgon Don't be absurd.

Elmire I don't mean a sexual or romantic love, although maybe it's that too, but love in the sense you can't live without him. What's in it for you, what does he give you?

Orgon He makes me feel safe.

Elmire From what? What do you of all people have to feel afraid of, look around you, at what you've got?

Orgon People used to be kind, now they're ugly, there used to be something to live for, now there's nothing, this country I helped build, the walls are crashing in around us.

Elmire What do you want? Where does this end?

Orgon I want things to be how they were when I was young.

Elmire When you were young!

Orgon That's what Tartuffe is offering, a return to a time when things meant something, where there was love and kindness, not cruelty and selfishness.

Elmire This is cruel, this is selfish.

Orgon It is tough but so is the world and she needs to learn that.

Elmire The world hasn't changed, you have. And now you want to change the world from how it is to how you remember it. But it wasn't different. You were different, you were less afraid and this is why the world keeps getting dragged back. Because men like you get old and scared.

How far you want to take us back? One hundred years? Two, three hundred, four? Drop a pin anywhere in history, go back a million years, you'd find early man, creating an entire belief system just to avoid admitting he's losing his hair. And four hundred years from now, people'll be telling this same story then too.

Cleante There's a bleak old thought.

Elmire Deep down, you all want the same thing, power or sex or both.

Orgon You're one to talk with all your visitors.

Cleante They are just visitors, Orgon.

Orgon You expect me to believe that.

Cleante That's enough. My sister has every right to have guests, there's nothing suspicious about it. So she has friends round, some of them are men, so what? She's shown you nothing but love and this is how you treat her, anything else is a sordid lie, I'm sorry, you don't deserve her.

Elmire No, not a lie.
  Some of them are lovers.
  Don't all look at me like that! It's been nearly a year since my husband so much as glanced at me and I have no intention of joining a convent or *Médecins Sans* bloody *Frontières*.
  What did you expect? When your old mates caught wind you were having a difficult time, you would not believe the number of 'Heys!' started popping up in my inbox – 'Hey! How is Orgon? And how are you?'
  So many decent men, all alive to the angle, it's so boring, so commonplace, so tiring fending them off.

Orgon My friends, I should have known.

Elmire Your friends? God no, I didn't sleep with your creepy friends, they're awful. No, I found people I actually liked.
There's some really nice people out there. Interesting, attractive, fun.

Orgon How many were there?

Elmire It's vulgar to count, and you know what? In the end, I just thought, why not? How come it's the men get to be all conflicted and confused, what about my fears, my insecurities, where's my mid-life crisis, when do I get to be the arsehole? When are my needs met?
Don't worry, everyone had a nice time and no animals were harmed.

Cleante Okay, that's not ideal.

Orgon Tartuffe was right about you, without an ounce of shame.

Elmire Oh fuck your shame. What, I should be the dutiful wife, all patient and wise while you have your spiritual embolism, throw your children's future away, wait for you to come back all chastened, having learnt something, grow up

Orgon All I can say is I'm glad I have Tartuffe to rely on.

Elmire You think he's different, my God, you still don't get it, do you, the delusion!

Orgon Of course he's different. He's Tartuffe!

Elmire What if I prove he's not who he seems?

Orgon Then I would know the proof to be false!

Elmire He's really done a number on you, hasn't he? Every lie he tells, every deception, every accusation he faces, it's just more fuel for the conspiracy! The worse he behaves, the more we accuse him, the more you're convinced we're out to get him, it's perfect!

And what I hate, what I resent is that despite all this, despite myself, I still love you.

The man I met, with the shy smile, the man I fell in love with, the man I married, was loving. He was generous. And passionate. And kind. I miss him. Is he there? Anything? A glimmer?

Orgon?

Orgon It's by our actions we are judged, not fine words.

Elmire I'll show you who your pal really is so you can *see* it, right in front of you.

Orgon Impossible.

Elmire Or are you so vain, so stupid, so insecure, you won't even trust the evidence of your own eyes any more?

What? Scared I might be right?

Orgon If you intend to humiliate yourself further, so be it. And when your plan fails, there will be no return. For you, nor anyone. She is not my daughter. And you are not my wife. Do you accept my terms?

Elmire Terms? You're offering me *terms*?

Cleante This is what Tartuffe wants, for you to put yourself in a position where you say something you can't take back.

Orgon Do you accept?

Elmire I do. But remember your own words, *there will be no return*, because there may not be any for you either.

Call Tartuffe. Tell him I'm alone.

Dorine What if he suspects something?

Elmire He'll be too preoccupied.

Cleante With what?

Elmire What he thinks he's getting.
  Out. It's not a bloody free-for-all.

  Dorine, Cleante and Mariane exit.

You. In there. Now.

Orgon I'm not getting in there.

Elmire Get in and stop complaining, hurry up.
  You asked for evidence, I'll give you evidence, and I
will only stop when you say the word.

Orgon Stop what?

Elmire The moment you're satisfied that Tartuffe has
sights on more than Heaven, you interrupt.
  And remember, whatever happens, I'm not doing it for
you, I'm doing it for your bloody children.

Orgon What exactly do you intend to do?

Elmire That all depends entirely on you.

  Enter Tartuffe.

Tartuffe You wish to see me?

Elmire *Fermez la porte, monsieur. Il y a des yeux
partout.*

Tartuffe I don't speak French.

Elmire Shut that door. We don't know who's watching.

  Tartuffe obliges.

Elmire The game's up.

Tartuffe I'm sorry, I don't know what you mean.

Elmire Oh come on, don't play that old tune, we both
know you saw through me from the start.

Tartuffe Saw through what?

Elmire When Damis walked in on us, a man of your perception must have noticed the lengths I went to stop him revealing all to my husband.

Tartuffe I assumed you were hoping to dissuade any interest I might have had in Mariane.

Elmire God, you're good.

Tartuffe I am? I mean, yes, I am.

Elmire I was so blinded by desire, I didn't see what you were doing, but the scales have fallen from my eyes, it's all so clear.

Tartuffe What is?

Elmire Marriage to Mariane was the perfect cover.

Tartuffe I'm sorry – cover for what?

Elmire Us, of course! With you as my son-in-law, no one would suspect a thing, least of all my husband, and that is why, without fear, I can open my heart – a heart all too ready to give in to your demands – and tell you that I want you like I have never wanted any man. Or woman for that matter.

Tartuffe The Lord really does move in mysterious ways. Perhaps too mysterious.

Elmire You're hesitant. Is it because I spurned you before? How fickle we women are, we barely know our own minds.
  Ah-hahahahaha!
  When you first made your proposition I was shocked. You touched a part of me that hadn't been touched in far too long.
  My heart!

Tartuffe Your heart, yes, I touched your heart!

Elmire I had trouble admitting the strength of my feeling. In refusing to yield, I was at war with my own nature.

Tartuffe You wanted to yield?

Elmire Why else would I have entertained your advances for so long before Damis so rudely interrupted?
  When I tried to persuade you to break off the marriage to Mariane, was it not obvious my true motive was to have you for myself?
  All us women need is a little push, a little nudge, a little coaxing in order to open up.

Tartuffe Your words are a cool breeze to my ears.

Elmire Do you like that?

Tartuffe Very much so.

Elmire Tell me you feel the same way I do.

Tartuffe Is it not apparent?

Elmire Forgive my craven desire for reassurance, but I really must hear the words.

Tartuffe The words?

Elmire Yes, the exact words, I'm afraid I'm a stickler for clarity, it's a thing of mine and I need to be absolutely clear that you would gladly betray my husband's trust for one hour in my arms.

Tartuffe Just the one hour?

Elmire Two!

Tartuffe Two and three quarters?

  Elmire coughs.

Elmire Can we just agree that you will betray my husband?

Tartuffe You want me to say that out loud?

Elmire I must be sure I'm not humiliating myself. What's wrong?

Tartuffe Your change of heart is a little abrupt.

Elmire The passion you arouse makes me impulsive.

Tartuffe We are alone, aren't we?

Elmire Of course.

Tartuffe eyes up Orgon's hiding place.

Look at me, I'm here, I'm here, why do you doubt me all of a sudden?

Tartuffe Perhaps something a little more tangible might persuade me of your sincerity.

Elmire What sort of thing you didn't mind mind?

Tartuffe Something to get the juices flowing for the banquet ahead.

Elmire Oh a food metaphor, how charming.

Tartuffe A mere appetiser would suffice.

Elmire It rather seems you're keen to head straight to the main.

Tartuffe Although what I really crave is my desserts!

Elmire coughs and evades Tartuffe.

That's a nasty cough.

Elmire It flares up at times of high stress.

Tartuffe Let me put you at ease.

Elmire coughs.

Elmire I'm so sorry, something seems to be stuck. If only it would shift.

Tartuffe It seems it's your turn to be hesitant.

Elmire It just pricks my conscience to put your salvation at risk in this way.

Tartuffe My salvation is not in question, now let no more pricks trouble your conscience.

Elmire I thought people like you had rules about this sort of thing.

Tartuffe More guidelines, actually.

Elmire coughs.

That cough really is quite persistent.

Elmire As are you.

Tartuffe I have heard of an old wives' remedy surprisingly effective in alleviating a sore throat.

Elmire A glass of water would do just fine – are you absolutely sure this is allowed?

Tartuffe Theologically speaking, I'm not even sure if it's really happening.

Elmire Is it not?

Tartuffe If a tree falls in a forest, and no one is there, does it really made a sound?

Elmire I don't follow.

Tartuffe In the same way, if two adults have a liaison, and no one else is the wiser, can it really be said to have happened?

Elmire Yeah, I'm pretty sure it can.

Tartuffe Look, do you want this or not?

Elmire Well it's not so much a question of want, more a question of whether anything can prevent it from happening. As far as I can see there are no further obstacles to you satisfying your – (*Coughing.*) every carnal impulse, your every – (*Terrible coughing.*) wanton desire, unless of course – (*Fearsome coughing.*) by some bloody miracle something were to come between us –

It seems we must make ourselves slaves to our lust!

Tartuffe Oh Elmire!

Elmire Wait!

Tartuffe WHAT IS IT NOW?

Elmire A noise.

Tartuffe Where?

Elmire Outside.

Tartuffe I heard nothing.

Elmire Open that door, check my husband isn't listening in.

Tartuffe No one is there.

Elmire Please, I can't possibly abandon myself if there is any distraction!

Tartuffe What would he be doing out in the corridor?

Elmire Waiting for an opportune moment to catch us in the act?

Tartuffe Orgon! He wouldn't suspect a thing! That man is such an idiot, we could make love right under his nose, he wouldn't even blink!

Elmire The thought had occurred to me.

   Tartuffe exits.
    Orgon emerges.

So soon? Are you sure?

Orgon I can't believe what I heard, the nerve of that man!

Elmire Now do you believe me?

Orgon He called me an idiot!

Elmire That's what bothers you? That he calls you an idiot?

Orgon I thought he was my friend, I trusted him, how could he say those things about me?
But you know what, I'm glad we saw through him in the end.

Elmire You know what, get back in there.

Orgon What?

Elmire Maybe you haven't had enough proof yet.

Elmire pushes Orgon back into his hiding place.
Tartuffe enters.

Tartuffe The coast is clear!

Elmire grabs Tartuffe, kisses him on the lips, turns him so that when Orgon appears from his hiding place, Orgon will not immediately be seen.
Tartuffe readies himself for ecstasy.

We are entering the realm of the senses! No boundaries! No limits!

Orgon appears, watches dumbfounded.

Now is God's appointed hour – he is coming!
The curtain is rent in twain!
Behold the mighty instrument of the Lord!

Tartuffe notices Orgon.

It's not how it looks.

Orgon Pack your bags, get out of my sight, never darken my hallways again.

Tartuffe I thought this was what you wanted!

Orgon To seduce my wife?

Tartuffe You told me to spend more time with her!

Elmire Did he now?

Tartuffe He insisted I spend time alone with you, said he wanted to get people talking.

Orgon But not actually have sex with her?

Tartuffe I was attempting no such thing.

Orgon So what was that?

Tartuffe Spiritual guidance.

Elmire You asked him to be alone with me?
    What am I in all this, some sort of currency? A bargaining chip?
    You think I enjoy this, you think I like being pawed by men like him in order to clean up after men like you, you think this is fun?

Orgon Can we do this another time?

Elmire No we fucking well can't.

Tartuffe Okay, I sense a lot of anger here, emotions are high, I feel there is some miscommunication, I suggest we all take time, reflect, see what we can learn from this whole misunderstanding.

Orgon I want you out of my house now!

Tartuffe Okay, let's not do anything rash.

Orgon You're nothing but a liar and a fraud.

Tartuffe Careful not to say anything you come to regret.

Orgon The only thing I regret is letting you through my doors in the first place.

Tartuffe I do your dirty work, this is how you treat me?

Elmire What dirty work?

Tartuffe Whipped the household into shape, instilled some morality in all this fucking decadence, stopped you all eating yourselves! I did everything you asked of me!

Elmire What do you mean, everything he asked of you?

Tartuffe He kept banging on about how you all needed discipline.

Elmire So this is your doing?

Orgon You told me you had gifts of the spirit, that you were special.

Tartuffe I am!

Orgon You are nothing of the sort.

Tartuffe You were the one told me I was!

Orgon Don't blame me!

Tartuffe I'd begun to doubt my calling, no one paid any attention to me, they berated me – I was a prophet without a country – then you came along and persuaded me I could hear from God, you convinced me! You! You! You!

Orgon You sat down next to me and started praying!

Tartuffe You looked lonely! I was being kind!

Orgon I refuse to hear another word, I want you out, you don't belong here, you hypocrite.

Tartuffe Hypocrite? Me?
    I'm not the hypocrite. I've never pretended to be anything I'm not, but you – you! Sitting here in all this wealth, forged off the back of your misdeeds, your dodgy deals, you're the hypocrite!

Enter Cleante.

Cleante What is all this?

Enter Dorine and Mariane.

Orgon Get out. I never want to see you again.

Tartuffe I'll go. For now.
But I'll be back to claim what's mine.

Exit Tartuffe.

Dorine
Finally.

Cleante
About bloody time.

Elmire
What did he mean, 'Claim what is mine'?
What did he mean by 'Claim what is mine'?

Mariane
Are you all right?

Orgon
I need to sit down.

Mariane
Daddy, answer me please.

Orgon
Suddenly feeling a little overwhelmed. A profound
   unease
In the pit of my gut.

Cleante
About what?

Orgon
My wife. My daughter. My son.

Mariane
Daddy, you're scaring me!

Dorine
Breathe! Breathe!

Elmire

                     Orgon, what the hell have you done?

Orgon

And now comes fear, no not fear – terror.
Oh God. I've made the most catastrophic error.

Five

Orgon, Cleante.

Cleante Let me get this straight, you did what?

Orgon It was a complicated period for the country, there were all sorts of deals going on, we all did things we weren't proud of.

Cleante I know, but most of us shredded the fucking evidence.

Orgon I couldn't bring myself to do it.

Cleante What were you thinking?

Orgon I felt guilty – maybe on some deep psychological level I wanted to be caught.

Cleante Maybe on some deep psychological level, you're an idiot.

Orgon This isn't helping.

Cleante The kind of deals we're talking about. This is serious. This is treason.

Orgon Stop saying that! It's not treason.
Oh God it is treason.

Cleante Let's look at the positives. It could be worse.

Orgon Could it?

Cleante Tartuffe is aware of the existence of these documents, correct?

Orgon Yes.

Cleante But he has no actual evidence. As long as he doesn't have evidence it's fine, it's not like you handed him the incriminating documents.

You handed him the incriminating documents.

Orgon I didn't know what else to do, I trusted him.

Cleante What possessed you?

Orgon He told me it was a necessary part of my spiritual development, that I had issues of control. I don't know! It made sense at the time.

Cleante What does my sister say to all this?

Orgon She's still not talking to me.

Cleante Do you blame her?

Orgon Cleante, please. You're my oldest friend. I need a calm, clear-headed assessment, unclouded by emotion. What are my chances? Be honest now.

Cleante An honest, calm, clear-headed, assessment.

Orgon Yes.

Cleante Unclouded by emotion.

Orgon Exactly.

Cleante You're totally fucked.

Orgon That's no use!

Cleante It's your fault for being so bloody stupid.

Orgon I'm not to blame, I'm the victim in all this!

Cleante Oh please.

Orgon Anyone could have been duped by him.

Cleante But somehow only you were.

Orgon Do you think he'll take the documents to the police?

Cleante No, he'll probably just blackmail you for all your money.

What did he mean by 'Claim what is mine'? Claim what? Your money?

Orgon Probably, I don't know. Look, we need to find a way of getting rid of him.

Cleante What we need is a miracle.

Enter Damis.

And we have Damis. Please. Join us.

Damis I just have.

Cleante Yes, it's a turn of – never mind.

Damis I came as soon as I heard.

Orgon Forgive me. The things I said – there is no excuse.

Damis Father, please, I don't blame you.

Cleante I do.

Damis Now is no time for recrimination.

Cleante For once, we agree.

Damis We must act and act fast! I have formulated a plan, brilliant in its simplicity.

Orgon Damis, I knew I could rely on you.

Cleante Well come on, let's hear it.

Damis The plan is . . . we kill Tartuffe.

Orgon We kill him?

Damis That's right.

Cleante Any more detail?

Orgon Damis, the ramifications, I mean for one we'd never get away with it.

Damis Ah, now this is the clever bit. We do get away with it.

Cleante And how do we get away with it?

Damis We get someone else to do the killing for us.

Damis gestures 'That's the plan' and waits for the reaction.
A beat. Damis repeats the gesture and again waits for the reaction.

Orgon And who is going to do the killing for us?

Damis Denizens of the street, cut-throats who inhabit a shady underworld where blood runs free and laws are mocked.

Cleante You know such men?

Damis Yes. I met them in a bar by the river. Reckless, desperate individuals with no morals, who'll do anything for cash, no questions asked.

Cleante Who are they?

Damis Out-of-work actors, mainly.

Cleante Have they done this sort of thing before?

Damis No, but they're really up for it. Except one of them has a callback to fall off a shed in *Holby* so he might have to bail but the rest are good to go.

Orgon No one is killing anyone.

Damis Why not?

Orgon We are honourable, enlightened people.

Damis You're right.

Orgon We don't resort to violence to get ourselves out of a hole.

Cleante No, we have lawyers for that sort of thing.

Orgon Exactly.

Pernelle, Mariane, Elmire enter.

Pernelle What absolute nonsense! Tartuffe simply isn't capable of such behaviour, this is a ruse! What does my son have to say on the matter?

Orgon I'm afraid it's true. He has deceived us all, he is entirely without scruples.

Pernelle Tosh and balls, I don't believe a word of it.

A doorbell.

Cleante Although to be fair, Tartuffe wasn't entirely culpable.
I mean technically what you did was entrapment.

Elmire Whose side are you on?

Cleante I'm just saying in a court of law –

Elmire We're not in a court of law.

Orgon No, but we could end up in one unless we think of something.

Pernelle You were all against him from the beginning, it's a conspiracy.

Orgon He has made fools of us all.

Elmire Speak for yourself.

Pernelle You always were prone to flights of fancy. As a boy you'd get an idea in your head and that was it, and this is no different, you've let this shower of dunces turn you against him.

Orgon I watched with my own eyes as he tried to put his hand on my wife's –

Pernelle On your wife's what?

Cleante Yes, that.

Pernelle He was probably trying to administer a blessing or sanctification of some sort.

Elmire Perhaps I should ask him to try it on you.

Orgon Why won't you believe me?

Mariane He won't really get Daddy arrested for treason, will he?

Orgon He couldn't!

Cleante To be fair, the law is on his side.

Orgon I don't want to be fair, what are we being fair for?

Cleante I'm not defending the man, but you have to hand it to him, what he's done is really quite ingenious, in some ways I almost admire him.

Orgon Stop being so reasonable.

Cleante It's the principle!

Elmire Fuck the principles, he's after our money.

Cleante We don't know what he wants.

Enter Dorine followed by Loyal and his staff.

Dorine He says he's got a court order, I couldn't keep him out.

Loyal Good day to you, sir. My name is Loyal, I'm here on matters relating to Mr Tartuffe.

Cleante Sorry, did you say your name was Loyal?

Loyal That's right.

Orgon That name rings a bell.

Cleante As in 'loyal'?

Loyal Yes, sir.

Cleante And are you?

Loyal We'll get to that.

Elmire I thought we might.

Loyal My old man was in your father's service for many years.

Orgon I knew that name was familiar.

Loyal Your father was good to my dad, supported him through thick and thin. My dad said to me, on his deathbed, 'Son – you ever get a chance to repay that family, you must,' so I consider it fate that I've been led here to perform this duty on this day.

Orgon Yes.

Loyal And in the light of this, in the name of justice, there is only one action I can take.

Orgon Which is?

Loyal To serve you with these papers. You and your family need to be out by the end of the day.
Sorry, I would've helped, but in the current economic climate it's more than my job's worth.

Elmire You're turfing us out of our own home?

Loyal Oh no, madam. Not your home. Mr Tartuffe's home.

Elmire What?

Loyal Your house belongs to him.

Cleante Since when?

Loyal Three minutes ago.
He registered the papers this morning.

Damis What papers?

Orgon The deeds to the house.

Elmire If he has the deeds to the house, they're fake. The house is ours and we have the deeds to prove it, don't we? Don't we?

Orgon I may have signed over the deeds of the house to him.

Elmire You did what?

Orgon I needed to shift all the money out of my account in order to safeguard it.

Elmire From what?

Orgon Some of my dealings may not have been entirely above board and apparently there were a few loose emails and there was an outside chance of the government seizing all my assets – it could have happened to anyone.

Cleante You signed the deeds of the house over to Tartuffe?

Damis This is quite bad, isn't it?

Cleante Yeah, it's not good.

Orgon What choice did I have?

Elmire You could have signed them over to me, or your children.

Orgon I didn't trust any of you!

Elmire You absolute prick.
Well, what am I supposed to say? Well done, have a balloon.

Cleante She's right you know, it is the sort of thing an absolute prick would do.

Elmire Anything else you neglected to tell us or is that it?

Orgon No, no, that's about it.

Loyal This feels like a family discussion, I might just leave you to it.

Elmire Wait! You can't do this.

Cleante He can. It's the law.

Elmire Then the law is absurd.

Pernelle I've a good mind to take those papers and jam them up your bottom.

Loyal If you do that, madam, I'll have you charged with perverting the course of justice.

Pernelle I am not a pervert!

Elmire And this is not justice!

Dorine Where's your compassion? Your decency? You spoke of loyalty and honour.

Loyal All right, because of the family connection, I can offer some leeway. You've got until midday tomorrow to vacate the property.

Cleante Your generosity knows no bounds.

Loyal I will have to insist a few of the lads stay the night, just to ensure everything's above board –

Cleante Lads, you say?

Loyal Don't worry, they're lovely fellas, no unspent convictions.

Cleante I'll be sure to keep a close eye.

Loyal Keys. If you don't mind.

Orgon hands the keys to Loyal.

Oh and – be lucky.

Loyal exits.

Dorine The poor man.

Pernelle Second I laid eyes on him, I knew that man Tartuffe was trouble, but did anyone listen?

Orgon Not now, Mother.

Elmire I need to sit down.

Cleante Well, now's the time, those chairs'll be gone tomorrow.

Enter Valere.

Valere It's me! Valere! I'm here to save the day!

Dorine Oh God.

Mariane Valere!

Valere Mariane.

Cleante Where did he spring from?

Valere There's not a moment to lose. I got a tip-off from an old chum in the CPS (I can vouch for him, he was my Fives captain at Durham). There's a warrant out for your arrest.

Orgon What's the charge?

Valere Treason.
    You'll be locked up as a common criminal, your name will be ruined, you'll have no way of ever challenging Tartuffe in court.

Damis And they might put your head on a spike!

Cleante You have to admit, it's very clever.

Elmire Cleante, when you and Tartuffe had your little tête-à-tête are you sure you didn't fall a little under his spell?

Cleante Don't be absurd, people like me don't fall for stuff like that.

Orgon This is it! My reckoning!

Valere Orgon, please. I've made arrangements. But you will have to go on the run. It won't be easy. You'll be an outlaw, a renegade, not sure where to turn or who to trust, with nothing to live off but your wits.

And this ten grand – honestly, it's nothing, just a little something to keep you going.

Mariane You told me you had no money!

Valere Not real money, I can spare ten grand though.

Orgon Forgive me, Valere, I misjudged you.

Valere All I ask in return, is your trust.

And that, Mariane – you'll reconsider your feelings for me.

Mariane I will. I have. I do.

Valere And to mark the occasion, I have composed a poem. It's called 'The Pigs Are After Me'.

The pigs are after me!
The pigs are after me!

Valere indicates this is the end of the poem.

Dorine Come on, before it's too late, get yourself going!

Valere and Orgon begin to leave.
Enter Tartuffe, with Officers.

Tartuffe Officers, this is the man of whom I speak.

Cleante Where do they keep coming from?

Elmire You're utterly devoid of conscience, aren't you?

Tartuffe I take no pleasure in this, it is my duty as a citizen.

Orgon I helped you when you had nothing!

Tartuffe To salve your own guilt at abandoning your family.

Mariane You're a liar and a fraud.

Tartuffe I'm the only honest man here.

Orgon You take my money. Evict me from my own home, try to seduce my wife and you have the brass clackers to claim to be honest?

Tartuffe
I claim what is mine by law.
Nothing less, nothing more.

Cleante
All those empty ministrations
About tearing down the foundations –
You're a fake and a fraud,
An imposter, nothing more.

Tartuffe
The time for talk is done.
Carry out your orders, son.

Officer
Very well then, sir, if you insist. I'm afraid you're nicked.

Tartuffe
What? Not me, him. There's been a mistake. You'll
    never make it stick.

Dorine
It seems crime really doesn't pay.

Officer
Now, If you wouldn't mind stepping this way.

Elmire
What's that thing you always say?
You know, before you pray.
I remember. *Namaste*.

Officer
You're going down for quite some time.

Tartuffe
But why? What's my crime?.

Officer
For starters, you stole from this family.

Tartuffe
Stole what?

Officer
The deeds.

Tartuffe
Surrendered willingly.

Officer
Judge sees it different I'm sorry to say.
Lads, if you don't mind, take him away.

Tartuffe
It's a stitch-up! I've been done!

Officer
Come on, pull the other one –
(Don't worry we'll bring him back when he's changed
his tune.)

Mariane
We're saved!

Damis
In the nick of time.

Elmire
And not a moment too soon.

Officer
He's known to us, and what's more,
He's done this kind of thing before.

Tartuffe
You can't do this, you've no right.

Officer
Sir, I'd strongly advise you not to fight,
It only ever makes it worse.
Unless you'd prefer to go home in an hearse.

Tartuffe
You can't do this, it's not in the script.

Officer
Maybe in your version some pages got ripped.

Tartuffe is dragged towards the exit by Officers.

Tartuffe
Stop this bloody rhyming, it's not fun any more.

Dorine
Could you try not to scuff the floor?
Getting rid of scratches is such a bore.

Officer
Sorry, would you mind opening that door?

Tartuffe
Enough!

Tartuffe breaks free, addresses the audience.

You can't let them do this to me.
I gave you flowers!

Orgon They can't help you.

Tartuffe
Why won't they come to my defence?

Damis Why would they?

Tartuffe They're my friends!

Elmire No, darling, just the audience.

Tartuffe is dragged off by Officers.

Orgon
What on earth just happened?

Mariane

       The most awful fright.

Elmire
For a moment there I thought he'd –

Cleante

         Quite.

Officer
News of your predicament reached the PM's ears
So she dispatched me here to allay your fears
And while she can't condone illegal schemes,
Your loyalty's been noticed, if you know what I mean.
She appreciates your support since the war
And turns a blind eye to what we just saw.
We've all done things of which we're not proud.

Cleante
I don't mean to carp but is this allowed?
I mean normally a man reaps what he sows.

Officer
Yes, but when push comes to shove we take care
 of our own.

Elmire
The PM has saved us in our hour of need.

Cleante
It's just that Tartuffe had the deeds.

Dorine
Be quiet!

Cleante
   Fair and square.

Elmire
    Darling, let's just leave it there.

Officer
    Common criminals terrorising the likes of you?
    Behaviour like that simply won't do.
    People start thinking they can redistribute wealth.

Pernelle
    Imagine the effect on one's health.

Officer
    I think you'll agree it's all for the best.

Cleante
    Is this legal?

Officer   Hm. More or less.

    *Officers bring Tartuffe back in, bloodied, horribly
    beaten.*

                                        Now. Confess.

Tartuffe The scales have fallen from my eyes.
    I have seen the light. I apologise.
    I return everything that is rightfully yours.
    I acknowledge the justice of your cause.
    Accept my full, unforced confession,
    Free from coercion or state oppression.
    And let my tale prove a salutary lesson to all
    That pride always precedes a fall.
    And for the safety and protection of this great nation,
    We must never get ideas above our station.

Officer
    Sign.

    Tartuffe signs.

Dorine
        Justice is seen to be done.

Orgon

                                Order restored!

Elmire

Ensuring peace and harmony for all.

Orgon

Dear friends, if you would, before we part –

Elmire

Seeing as the storm seems to have passed –

Orgon

We must turn to matters of the heart.

Mariane

Valere.

Valere

           Mariane.

Dorine

                       Reunited at last.

Damis

And please –

Pernelle

             As we take our leave –

Cleante

                             Let us dwell on the universal law –

Orgon

One rule for the one per cent –

Tartuffe

                           And another for the poor.

But if you will – just before you shuffle from your seats,
Through the foyer, out into the cold and empty streets
Of London – city of riches, poverty, and all other
    extremes –

Turn your mind to those less fortunate, those like me.
And later still, in the warmth of your beds, consider
    this
Strange and troubling thought, one not so easily
    dismissed,
That you know, in the unsettled silence, to be the truth –

*Tartuffe gestures to his acolytes, who surround the
stage now, enveloping the action, encroaching steadily
on the audience.*

A reckoning comes. Expect us. For we are all Tartuffe.